TO SEE OURSELS

Rural Scotland in Old Photographs

Dorothy I Kidd

Photographs selected by
Alison Cromarty and
Dorothy I Kidd

HarperCollins*Publishers*

NATIONAL MUSEUMS OF SCOTLAND

HarperCollins Publishers, PO Box,
Glasgow G4 0NB
National Museums of Scotland,
Chambers St, Edinburgh EH1 1JF

First Published 1992

ISBN 0 00 470098 8

Reprint 9 8 7 6 5 4 3 2 1 0

A catalogue record for this book is
available from the British Library

Printed in Hong Kong

CONTENTS

Haymaking at Rackwick on Westray in Orkney, in the 1930s. This photograph, taken by local photographer William Hourston, shows the writer

H V Morton filming the old man, perhaps watched by another photographer.
William Hourston, Stromness

PREFACE

Photographs like these take us to the heart of our immediate past. So often we can recognise the people in them as just like ourselves, or at least like people we see every day. Who can enjoy the images of the lads playing marbles (with the dog waiting to pounce - p.121), or of the little girls at their doll's tea party (p.122) without feeling the years roll back to a universal experience of childhood? At other times, the strangeness of the picture emphasises that one age is not always like another, and that few now feel the intensity of certain things that moved our forebears: consider the congregation at the outdoor preaching at Lochcarron, so intent, so pious and so grim (p.104). In pictures of the old we seem to see kindly familiar faces, but how much more shrunken and gap-toothed than the elderly today, and we appreciate what late 20th-century dental care, and dentures, have done to our appearance.

Many who enjoy this book will recall from its photographs the working methods, the tools and the vehicles which surrounded them when they were younger, and see again in the countryside the pride of work in the age of the horse and the early tractor, of the scythe, the sheaf and the thatched home. It can be a shock to see that an old picture was taken in 1961 rather than in 1911, so uneven has been the pace of change in different parts of the country, at least until 30 years ago. Older pictures show us a world beyond memory but not beyond fellow feeling: how will the Misses Duncan in the Rover Landaulette (p.94) keep those hats on in the Scottish wind, unless they are riveted to their very heads with unseen pins?

Studying photographs conveys an untold wealth of detail in social history, and raises all sorts of odd questions. How could fishermen lay out their catches on the quay in Stornoway (p.50) without a horde of gulls coming to steal them? Were there fewer gulls then? Some plates, like the one of a Lewisman plucking young gannets (p.70), show an activity so old that it connects with the sea world of the Vikings. Others, like the aircraft on the beach (p.101) remind us that 20th-century technology ages quickly.

This volume is, we hope, the first of several that will show the extraordinary wealth of the Scottish Ethnological Archive. A new museum is being built which will use many more photographs as illustrative material in the galleries. But even that will only be the tip of the iceberg. The Archive itself, founded with such scholarly imagination by Alexander Fenton in 1959, is available for the public to study as one of the resources maintained by the National Museums of Scotland. This book gives just a taste of what can be found within.

T C Smout
February 1992

Watch the camera! Local children
and a visitor, photographed by
Robert Sturgeon, the postmaster on
the island of Coll, Argyllshire, in the
early 1900s.
Robert Sturgeon, Coll

INTRODUCTION

O wad some Pow'r the giftie gie us
To see oursels as others see us!

'To a Louse', Robert Burns

To See Oursels is a collection of memorable images of life in rural Scotland over nearly a century. Most were taken from the 1880s onwards when technical improvements in photography gradually made this hitherto expensive and complex medium affordable to all but the poorest. Photographs enable us to recreate a picture of the past and provide us with important evidence for our understanding of social history. Their value, both as historical documents and as a means of recording the present, is immense.

In the context of the artefacts from the past that feature in museum collections, country houses and heritage sites of all kinds, photographs can play a significant role. Many of the photographs included here show objects in use similar to those held in the collections of the National Museums of Scotland, and of many local museums. Very occasionally, we are also lucky enough to have a photograph of the actual object itself being used. Such photographs bring life to the objects and, more importantly, to the people who used them. They show us how and why an object was used, by whom, where, when and in what conditions. Together with very valuable, but unfortunately sometimes rather rare, first-hand accounts, photographs help us to a much clearer understanding of the lives of people in the past. They can preserve an object's human context which is so easily lost in a static exhibition.

Often photographs are the only visual evidence we have of much that may have disappeared, either through deliberate destruction such as the dismantling of redundant farm buildings, or through inevitable deterioration over time - working clothes and the clothes of poorer people are a good example here. Costume collections are frequently rich in people's best clothes and in the clothes of the wealthy, but they are quite unable to preserve clothes which have been worn until they are thrown out or turned into rags. Photographs, too, show how people wore their clothes, and how their clothes affected the shape of the body, in a far more direct way than either a dressed dummy or a dress designer's illustration.

Photographs are also a valuable guide to what people consider worthy of photographing and preserving. That in itself makes them revealing historical documents. Comparison between what different generations find worthy of recording can be extremely illuminating but it also underlines the principal drawback of photography as an historical tool. Something that must always be borne in mind when studying photographs is that they only record what the photographers want them to record. Care must therefore be taken when 'reading' a photograph. In the First World War Women's Land Army photograph included in the chapter on community life, for example, the women are in their dress uniform, not the clothes they actually used daily to work in. Without this kind of knowledge, photographs alone can be confusing. The information that accompanies a photograph – its own history – is therefore also important to our understanding of the past. The final chapter includes an example of the misunderstandings that can occur when a photograph is wrongly identified.

Since the earliest days of photography the tendency has been to use it to capture happy and striking events and people, and, generally, neither the everyday and mundane nor the extreme experiences of our lives. It is really only journalistic photography which covers areas such as warfare, bereavement, poverty or violence. If we are taking photographs ourselves, or commissioning a professional to do so, it will almost invariably be to record happy or significant personal or public occasions – a wedding, an outing, a family reunion or a civic ceremony. These and similar events, we may wish to document not only for personal or family reasons, but also because they give us status or help to identify us as belonging to a particular group – school groups, photographs of a workforce or of a person dressed in their best or in uniform, are good examples. In the first decades of popular photography it was very common to have photographs printed as postcards which could be sent to friends and relatives. Not unnaturally, these usually show people looking their best and in their best clothes.

An exception perhaps to the photographs taken only at happy and memorable times, are those taken partly subconsciously to guard against the time when the person photographed may no longer be alive. Many photographs of young servicemen and women, taken at the beginning of both World Wars, were probably taken for this reason as well as from a natural sense of pride.

Our lack of interest in recording the mundane and the everyday in photographs means that large parts of our lives are greatly under-represented by the photographic record. One such area is domestic life, and in particular the part played by generations of women in ensuring that homes operated smoothly. This omission may partly be due to the difficulties of indoor photography up to about the 1920s, but to a very great degree it is simply that we do not feel domestic life is worthy of recording. Fortunately, much of the work being undertaken today by local museums, and oral history groups in particular, is helping to redress this imbalance. And individuals can help too, by recording their own lives in words and photographs as completely as possible.

Happily, however, there are many photographs that do show the lives of ordinary people, doing everyday things. For this, we owe a debt to individual photographers – many of them tourists and amateurs, and now forgotten – who had the foresight to realise that everyday activities were also worthy of recording. Some of the major collections in this category held by the National Museums and used in this book are detailed below. We also owe much to the subjects of the photographs themselves, ordinary people who commissioned the many early photographers who travelled around the countryside (often on their bicycles) to take their photographs in their working environment, in family groups or at play.

All the photographs and quotations included in this book are from the Scottish Ethnological Archive in the National Museums of Scotland. Most of the photographs have been either donated to, or purchased by, the Archive, or lent for copying by individual owners. A few were copied from the photographic collections of other institutions. The quotations are taken from material lodged in the Archive's Manuscript Collection as a result of fieldwork and correspondence undertaken by curators over the past 33 years. The Archive also relies heavily on interested people providing both information and artefacts for its continuing growth.

The Archive was founded in 1959 by Alexander Fenton, the first curator of the Country Life collections in the then National Museum of Antiquities of Scotland, and now Professor of Ethnology at Edinburgh University. Its aims are to record and preserve documentary and illustrative material as context to the social history collections of the National Museums, and to provide a research tool for museum staff and public alike. Its remit is to document and illustrate the agricultural, rural, maritime, urban and industrial life of Scotland from the 17th century to the present day. Unusually for a museum collection, it contains not only original material but also copies and extracts from original sources. This provides a breadth of information not normally available in a single repository. The Archive also aims to maintain contact and collaborate with other Scottish museums and archives, in particular in order to spread the huge task of recording contemporary life in Scotland. In addition, this allows it to direct enquirers to the appropriate sources when unable to provide information itself.

The collection consists of photographs, slides, postcards and film; drawings and maps; audio tapes; manuscript sources such as diaries and account books; references to the objects relevant to the Archive's remit held in the National Museums' collections; newspaper cuttings, bibliographies and notes extracted from documentary and printed sources. It is arranged by subject, such as fish curing or grain thrashing, and each subject is then organised by county and parish order. Its photographic content makes the Scottish Ethnological Archive a major national photographic archive, complementing the Scottish Photography Archive maintained by the National Galleries of Scotland.

In the photographs included here, the photographers are always named where they are known. All known individuals are also named, always going from left to right of the photograph. Place names are spelt as they are on the Ordnance Survey 1:50 000 series. County names are included in the captions only when it is felt they contribute to identifying locations. Should any readers be able to help identify unnamed people or places, or wish to contribute to the Archive's collections, we should be very pleased to hear from them.

The following brief notes give details of the major collections in the Scottish Ethnological Archive from which many of the photographs in this book are drawn.

William Easton Collection – an important collection of photographic negatives taken by St Monance professional photographer William Easton between about 1890 and 1920. It shows life in the Fife fishing villages, and in St Monance in particular.

H B Curwen Collection – a collection of photographic negatives taken by H B Curwen between 1901 and 1904. They include photographs of life on Foula, Shetland, and photographs of sculptured crosses and churches in northern and western Scotland.

Cathcart Collection – a collection of photographs of life in the Uists taken from about 1897 to 1904.

Robert Sturgeon Collection – Robert Sturgeon, born at Dalbeattie in Ayrshire, came to the island of Coll, Argyllshire as postmaster in 1889. He worked there until his retirement in 1942. A keen photographer, he was very interested in photographing life on the island. His collection consists of glass plate negatives taken between about 1890 and 1910. It has been copied into the Scottish Ethnological Archive, and the original negatives returned to the island.

Mary Ethel Muir Donaldson (MEMD) Collection – born in Surrey in 1876 of a Scottish family, MEMD visited Scotland annually as an adult, and eventually came to live here permanently. She designed and built herself a house at Sanna in Ardnamurchan in 1925 and lived there until it was gutted by fire in 1947. She then moved to Edinburgh.

She travelled extensively in northern and western Scotland and wrote on Scottish history, and Scottish church history in particular on which she held strong views. She was also a skilled photographer, and seems to have specialised in topographical scenes and in portraits of her neighbours at Sanna, of people in Morar and Arisaig, and of the people she met on her travels.

Her collection of glass negatives and original prints was split after her death and is now housed in the collections of Inverness Museum and Art Gallery and in the Scottish Ethnological Archive. Particularly interesting amongst the SEA collection is a series of photographs recording the building of Sanna Bheag, her home in Ardnamurchan.

Alasdair Alpin MacGregor Collection - Alasdair Alpin MacGregor was born in mainland Inverness-shire in 1898. He was brought up there and later in Edinburgh. He joined the Seaforth Highlanders in 1915 and fought in France during the First World War. On being demobilised, he took an Arts degree at Edinburgh University where he developed strong anti-vivisectionist, teetotal and vegetarian views.

He spent most of his life as a freelance writer and photographer, travelling, photographing and writing about Scotland, and the Hebrides in particular. He was a frequent contributor to *Country Life* and one of his most interesting and moving assignments must have been when he was *The Times* correspondent for the evacuation of St Kilda in 1930.

He had a particularly romantic view of Scotland and of Gaeldom especially, which too often the real people whom he met, rather than the ones in his imagination, could not live up to. This led to controversy over some of his published works. The Lewis Association, for instance, was moved to publish a booklet entitled *The Western Isles - A Critical Analysis of the book of that name by Alasdair Alpin MacGregor* as a means of 'countering the attack on the good name of the people of the Hebrides', shortly after the book's publication in 1949.

Following his wishes after his death in 1970, his widow donated his photographic collection and a complete set of his published works to the National Museums. His personal papers are held by the National Library of Scotland.

It was one of Alasdair Alpin MacGregor's stipulations that his name should be spelt 'correctly and in full' with any publication of his photographs. This wish has been respected here.

***Scotland's Magazine* Collection** - *Scotland's Magazine* was published between 1928 and 1975, first as the *SMT Magazine* of the Scottish Bus Group, and latterly by the Scottish Tourist Board. The magazine published illustrated articles on working life, leisure, famous places and people and also kept in touch with technological developments in Scotland.

Upon privatisation of the Scottish Bus Group in 1989, a very large collection of photographs and a complete set of *Scotland's Magazine* were donated to the Archive. The photographs were taken between the late 19th century and 1975, although the majority date from the 1950s and 1960s - a period until then relatively poorly covered by the Archive, as potential donors tend to think that museums are not interested in the recent past.

Although we have tried to trace the photographers who took pictures for *Scotland's Magazine*, so far this has proved impossible. The publication of some photographs which may still be protected by copyright could therefore not be avoided. The Archive would be very interested to hear from any *Scotland's Magazine* photographers who may be able to provide further information on their work.

David Innes Collection – a professional photographer, who did much work with his wife for *Scotland's Magazine*. He bequeathed his large photographic collection to the National Museums. This collection is particularly strong in photographs taken between the 1930s and 1950s, concentrating especially on working life in Scotland.

Material copied from the following archives has also been included:

MacGrory Collection, Argyll and Bute District Libraries – this collection consists of nearly 3000 glass negatives taken in the 1890s and early 1900s by two brothers living in Campbeltown, Charles and Dennis MacGrory. Most are of people and places in Campbeltown and Kintyre, but there are also scenes from elsewhere in Scotland, and from France, Belgium, Italy and Ireland. The negatives were presented to Argyll and Bute District Library Service in 1977 by Charles's son, Anthony P MacGrory, and the collection is held in Campbeltown Public Library. The Scottish Ethnological Archive has been helping Campbeltown Library by making copy negatives and prints of the collection.

St Andrews University – the photographic collections of St Andrews University contain over 300,000 images, which date from specimens by William Henry Fox Talbot, the inventor of the negative/positive process to the present day. Major parts of the collection are the negatives of Valentine & Sons, Dundee, photographic publishers, 1860-1970, the negatives of Robert Moyes Adam (1885-1967), and the negatives of George Cowie, a press photographer who worked in the north of Fife, from 1929 to 1982. There are a dozen smaller archives within the collection. Between them most aspects of Scottish life are covered although there are relatively few images of Scottish heavy industry.

School of Scottish Studies – the School of Scottish Studies Photographic Archive is an important collection of over 10,000 prints and slides, and a growing number of films and video tapes. The collection records the results of field research since 1951. It reflects the research and teaching interests of the staff, including pastoral, agricultural and fishing activities, domestic life, vernacular buildings, crafts, industries and traditional practices. There is an emphasis on photographs of people doing things, and of the faces of the people of Scotland.

Scottish Photography Archive - the Scottish Photography Archive is a department of the National Galleries of Scotland. It was set up in 1984 to collect photographs as fine art in line with the Galleries' general policy. Mostly as a result of great public generosity, the collection now holds over 20,000 photographs, predominantly by Scottish photographers or taken in Scotland from the 1840s to the present. The Archive undertakes research used for publications and exhibitions as a basis for the historical and critical approach to photography. There is an annual programme of exhibitions and the photographs may be seen by appointment in the Print Room.

Scottish Photography Archive, Scottish National Portrait Gallery, Queen Street, Edinburgh EH2 1JD. Telephone 031-556 8921.

Walter Cunningham sowing by hand from a hopper at Holehousemuir Farm, south of Slamannan in Stirlingshire, April 1976. His right and left hands alternately grab a handful of seed and cast it up to nine feet forward in an arc as he walks. Prior to sowing, the ground had been ploughed and harrowed. Afterwards the seed was harrowed in. An acre was sown and harrowed in an hour.

This photograph is one of a series taken by the National Museums as part of a survey of hand-sowing. It is particularly interesting as it shows hand-sowing surviving until very recently in an, albeit isolated, part of Scotland's central belt.

LIVING WITH THE LAND

The invention and development of photography coincided with the enormous changes taking place in Scotland's agriculture from the early 19th century, and numerous photographers were able to pass on a visual record of how different farming practices and technical improvements altered Scotland's rural landscape. The photographs in this chapter focus on these changes, on traditional areas of farm work, on some more recent developments and on areas in which the National Museums' collections are particularly strong.

Mechanisation of the harvest, for instance, started with Patrick Bell's reaping machine in the 1830s, continued with the binder from the 1890s, and culminated with the combine harvester which reached Scotland in 1932. The power behind these machines altered dramatically. Before the introduction of petrol-driven tractors during the First World War, horses provided the principal motive power on farms. Between the wars, the use of tractors spread, and by the 1960s had completely replaced the horse. One major consequence of mechanisation was the huge reduction in the workforce required on farms.

An example of an area in which the National Museums' archival collections are strong, is the pig-killing and curing survey undertaken throughout Scotland in the early 1970s. Unlike the other animals reared on farms which were productive before slaughter, pigs were reared exclusively for the meat and skin they would provide. Because of the increased importance placed on meat in the diet, from the mid-19th century many farm workers bought young pigs and fattened them up for home-killing, curing and consumption during the winter months.

The traditional processing of dairy produce on the farm has also tended to disappear with mechanisation and much stricter hygiene laws. Until the Second World War, most farms and crofts made enough butter and cheese for their own needs, with perhaps some left over for sale. In marked contrast to other agricultural pursuits, commercial poultry-keeping and soft-fruit growing are 20th-century developments. Until the end of the 18th century, hens tended to be regarded by farmers as a nuisance. During the 19th century, poultry-keeping gradually increased, but it was not until the 1920s that technical improvements in poultry management produced a significant rise in poultry-keeping and egg production.

Commercial soft fruit production took off in Scotland at the end of the 19th century. This was due mainly to the increased demand for fresh fruit and jam; but in Perthshire and Angus the industry also developed in part as a response to the depression in the local spinning and weaving industries.

James Frame, pausing in his ploughing, on the estate of Craigthornhill
near Hamilton, in about 1904. The
man behind him is spreading
fertiliser with the help of a sowing
hopper.

Mr Tait ploughing with a German-
built, four-wheel-drive MAN tractor
at Broachrigg Farm, Rosewell,
Midlothian, in late 1951 or 1952.
The tractor, sold to him by the new
Scottish Agricultural Industries agricultural machinery and implement
depot at Haddington, did not prove
as popular in Scotland as hoped.
However, this one worked well for
many years and, since the sale of Mr
Tait's farm, has been bought and
restored by a private collector.

Mr Bruce proudly demonstrating his
first tractor – the popular, reliable
and relatively inexpensive Fordson –
at Overside of Fergus, near St Fergus
in Aberdeenshire. He sold two
horses and two carts in order to buy
the tractor for £200 in 1919.

Harvesting at Fletcherfield Farm near Kirriemuir, about 1932. This scene is fascinating because it shows both the old and the new. Two binders are being pulled by three horses each; and a third by an American International 10-20 tractor. This was one of the first tractors to be used in Angus, and a popular model during the 1920s and 1930s.

Eck Fotheringham is driving the tractor, with Pete Mitchell behind him on the binder. The man, almost totally concealed by the sheaves he is carrying, and the two men on the right, are building the bound sheaves into stooks.

Cutting badly lying corn with sickles near Lamington, about six miles south-west of Biggar, around the 1880s or 1890s. The leather strap, seen looped around the wrist of the man on the right, was attached to the handle of the sickle and provided additional support. The man in the centre has a sharpening stone tucked into his belt. The men may well have been migrant Irish shearers who had come over for the harvest.

An Oliver combine harvester at work, photographed probably about the 1940s. It is being pulled by a barely-visible Fordson tractor. Once cut and thrashed, the corn was bagged and deposited in the sack discharge seen on the left.

Answering a question, in a survey conducted by the NMS, on the time saved by a combine over a tractor and binder, two farmers commented as follows: James McAlister of Bruchag Farm on Bute wrote: 'From one week with the combine, from 5 to 6 weeks with the binder', and Duncan McAlister of Kerrytonlia Farm, also on Bute, wrote: 'A 10 ft combine will harvest 1 acre in 45 minutes. Tractor-binder will take 1 hour to cut 1 acre, 2 men 1½ hours to stook same, 8 hours to cart and stack, 3 hours to thresh. Total 13½ hours.' Both these farms acquired their first combines in the early 1960s.

The staff at Gleghornie Farm, near North Berwick, photographed during the harvest of 1938. They are (back row) James Montgomery, Willie Allan, Leslie Oliver, Willie Allan jnr and John Allan; (centre row) Willie White, Jock White, Ted Allan, Pringle Bolton, Harry White, John Shiel, Eck Renton and two Irish workers; (front row) Will Hendry, Jean White, Mary Johnstone, Mary Allan, Helen Johnstone, Chris Bolton and Agnes Blacklock. At this period the farm kept six pairs of horses, employed about twenty staff and had eight cottages, some occupied by four or five workers. Today there are three tractors and one full-time employee who is helped as required by a few casual staff and contractors using modern machinery. He lives in one of the cottages. The others are let as holiday homes.

Binders at work in Angus, possibly around the 1940s. Binders, which appeared in the late 19th century, were an improvement on mechanical reapers as they incorporated an attachment which tied each sheaf of grain as it was cut, thus dispensing with a time-consuming and back-breaking task, previously carried out by hand. Pulling a binder was one of the hardest tasks for horses, especially when a wet summer had made the grain heavy and the ground soft. Then extra motive power was required and three rather than two horses would be yoked to the binder (as can be seen here). For large crops, two or more binders would work together to save time.

Stacking hay at West Windygoul
Farm, Tranent, in 1923. The pole
protruding from the hay on the right
is part of a hay-lifter, a device
invented in the early 1900s to help
in the work of stack building.
A system of pulleys allowed large
amounts of hay to be winched up in
a single operation. Here it is being
attached to the contents of a cartload
of hay. Despite this improvement,
large numbers of people were still
required to help during haymaking.
Other implements being used are
forks and rakes.

Smiling farm workers, including two female outworkers, photographed during thrashing operations in Roxburghshire, or possibly Northumberland in the early 1900s.

They are preparing sheaves for thrashing, almost certainly in a steam-powered travelling mill which is out of the photograph. Sheaves were untied just before thrashing. The resulting grain was bagged, and the straw and chaff baled or stacked. Today, thrashing is carried out at the same time as the crop is cut by the combine harvester.

Both women are wearing the distinctive protective bonnets or *uglies* of female outworkers in the Lothians and Borders.

Scything at Ness on the north tip of the island of Lewis in the 1950s or 1960s. Tractor-driven mowers have since replaced the scythe, but oats are still tied into sheaves by hand today. Both men and women used sickles for shearing grain crops, but scythes were used only by men because of the additional strength required to wield them.

Hoeing and singling turnips at Ormiston Mains Farm, Ormiston, East Lothian, in 1933. The squad have paused in their task of slowly working their way up the turnip drills, weeding and thinning out the young plants. The appearance of the photographer has given them the opportunity to rest their backs and shoulders. Note that the woman is wearing a cap designed principally to keep the hair clean during domestic work, rather than to protect her from the sun during outdoor work.

Planting seed potatoes in March 1953, the locality unknown. The clever use of potato sacks, adapted as hoppers, allowed the women to keep both hands free for planting and reduced the weight of the load.

Although potato planting has since largely been mechanised, harvesting still requires additional hands.
Robert M Adam Collection, St Andrews University

Potato dressing at West Pilton Farm, near Davidson's Mains to the west of Edinburgh, in 1912 or 1913. The potatoes are being riddled to shake out the very small ones, and then graded according to size and quality. This task requires large numbers of workers. Potato baskets, made of thin strips or spales of wood, retained their shape which fits cosily onto the hip, even after they were made of modern materials. All but one of the women are wearing *uglies*, and wrist or armguards to keep their blouses clean.

A difficult calving for an Ayrshire heifer at Bass Rock Farm, near North Berwick, in 1976. The men are: head dairyman John Elliot, the Haddington vet, Mr Chawner, Dick MacAdam, grieve, and Ian, a farm worker from North Berwick. The farm was well known for its poultry and dairy cattle and provided a milk round in North Berwick. It was sold off in the late 1970s and the land has since been built over.
Morven Wright

Mrs Pirie proudly posing next to a wooden rack on which her home-made cheeses are drying at Orphir on the mainland of Orkney in 1961. The cheeses pictured here were pressed using a Don press, a spring-loaded press introduced during the Second World War which applied greater pressure than earlier presses and therefore extracted more whey. Two bags of curds like the one hanging to the right of the photograph were placed together in the press to make the cheese. Note the net placed over the cheeses to protect them from pests.
Alexander Fenton, NMS

At work with a milk-bottling machine, possibly in Perthshire in the 1960s. A roll of metal foil, used to produce disk-shaped seals for the bottles, can be seen whole at the top of the machine and used in the per-forated strip.

After the creation of the Scottish Milk Marketing Boards in 1933, milk producers, hauliers and distri-butors were gradually able to invest in better equipment for milking, storing and processing a product which had to be handled as hygieni-cally as possible.

Hand-milking on North Uist in the 1950s. The woman's polka-dot overall beautifully picks up the markings on the cow. Unfortunately, neither the woman nor the exact location have been identified.

Cows, which were traditionally milked from the right, occasionally require some form of restraint to stop them kicking, but here the trust between milkmaid and cow seems complete. Lady Maitland of Reswallie, who helped set up the Angus Folk Museum at Glamis, described how when she was a child her cow was restrained: 'I had my own little luggie to milk into and if my cow would not stand still, she had a broomstick leant against her so she was afraid to move in case it fell.'

Mrs Brown, the housekeeper, making butter at Brownhill Farm, Auchterless, Aberdeenshire, in 1962.

Above, she is pouring off the buttermilk (a by-product of churning cream into butter) from the barrel-churn. The butter is then worked with butter hands and made into decorative pats and interesting shapes, possibly for the entertainment of the fascinated child, Eilene Fenton.

Mrs Margaret MacMillan from Ayrshire described her family's first barrelchurn, acquired around 1900: 'Our next model was the end over end, barrel shaped. It was a bit easier to use but had to be kept turning away for about 15-20 minutes. The barrel had a small glass window on the lid (removed in the photograph) and one could see when the butter was ready.'
Alexander Fenton, NMS

Perhaps Mrs Maclean, making butter using a plunge churn at Sorisdale on the island of Coll, Argyllshire, in the 1890s or 1900s. Recalling helping her grandmother to churn in the 1900s at Roadside of Auchinderran, near Keith in Banffshire, Annie Stirling Stronach said: 'Churning was done in a plump-churn, with a lid. The "plumper" [plunger] had a round-about head with holes in it. In very hot weather if the butter would not come, grannie whiles put in a grain of salt. Three days' milk usually kept for churning, on an average. After we churned we used to get a piece - she just took a bit of loaf and spread it with a "thoom fae" o' butter, taken straight out of the churn on her thumb. When the butter came you just washed your hands and lifted it out, then worked it in cold water till all the buttermilk was out of it. Buttermilk put in a jar and kept for baking, or might be drunk in part.'
Robert Sturgeon, Coll

Watched by her son, a woman rests her back during hand–clipping on the island of Flotta in Orkney in 1924. She is using spring-tined shears of the type adopted during the 19th century as replacement for the slower scissor shears. Spring-tined shears are still used today on occasions when electric shears are not practical. The sheep's legs are tied together to immobilise it.
William Hourston, Stromness

The old and the new at Glentennet, about two miles to the north of Tarfside in Glen Esk, Angus, in 1968. The man in the foreground is using traditional hand shears, while behind him a row of sheep are being shorn with electrically-powered shears. The cables leading from shears to engines can be seen dangling from the wooden beam from which the engines were suspended.

Although the first mechanical sheep clippers appeared early in the 1900s, it was not until they could be powered by electricity that machine clipping began to spread. In hill areas where electricity might not be available, hand clipping remained the rule until well into the second half of the 20th century.

A group of women and schoolgirls holding bundles of flax, photographed in Fife in about 1915. They may have been sent to help pull the flax crop during the First World War, although their dress, including small bunches of the tiny bright blue flax flowers in many of their hats, looks more like a fashion show. Flax has to be pulled either by hand, or much more recently by machine, rather than cut, in order to prevent damage to the fibres and to preserve their maximum length.

The 18th century was the great period for flax growing in Scotland; and eastern and south-west Scotland were the areas where the linen industry was most developed. But small quantities were grown in many areas up until the 1950s, following a revival during the Second World War. The advent of synthetic fibres and cheaper foreign imports, however, seemed to have killed off the industry, until flax growing was revived in Angus in the 1980s, in part as a means of agricultural diversification.

Men demonstrating bristle scrapers used in pig-killing, at Rumbleton Farm, Greenlaw, Berwickshire, in about 1910; the man on the left wears a leather pouch to hold the various knives needed.

W Smith wrote about pig-killing in Aberdeenshire in the early 1900s: 'Following the killing the pig was allowed a short time to bleed and then taken to the barrel which was partly filled with hot water... it (the pig) had to be kept turning until hair, scruff and even the hooves were easily removed. When it reached that stage it was lifted out and laid on what was usually a door set on trestles or such like. Then the final cleaning took place, scraping off hairs etc, and finally douched with cold water... It was now taken to some place indoors where it was hung up by the hind legs, and the entrails removed and allowed to drop into a tub placed directly under the animal's head. The trotters were removed later when the carcase was left to hang for a day or two until the flesh had sufficiently become firm.'

This photograph shows the hanging of a pig carcase, somewhere in Fife between about 1910 and 1920. The little boy is holding a balloon presumably made from the pig's bladder.

Mr Smith goes on to describe the cutting up of the carcase and both the wet curing in brine and the dry curing with salt, saltpetre and spices. Curing was principally carried out by the women. Interestingly, although children seem to have been included in the excitement of the first stages of the pig-killing and curing, women are not recorded here and may have kept out of the way until later on.

Hen-feeding and egg-gathering at Stonelaws Farm near Haddington in the 1920s. Recalling the development of poultry-keeping in Aberdeenshire, Mabel Smith wrote: 'In the old days hens had to be "cruived" (put into hen-coops) at seed-time and at harvest if a corn field was near. This meant a dearth of eggs for a time, as nobody would have thought it worth while at such busy times to give the hens anything to compensate for their loss of freedom. During the Second World War, owing to scarcity of food, many men took to egg production on a large scale and from then on, it became a business proposition, not just a side-line for the farmer's or cottar's wife to bring in a little money for housekeeping.'

Canning raspberries in a Montrose factory in 1957. Here the women are checking that the correct weight of raspberries has gone into each tin. Syrup is then added, before the air is extracted and the tins sealed.
P K McLaren, Perth

Raspberry-picking at Burnhead Farm, Blairgowrie, in the 1920s or 1930s. It would be fascinating to know the identity of the well-dressed gentleman carrying the briefcase.

Mrs M McNicoll, whose father started growing raspberries at Knowhead Farm near Kirriemuir in Angus in 1904, wrote: '...the industry grew, till by 1914, it was a thriving one, employing pickers in July and August, mostly mothers with children from the Town and Southmuir. No outside pickers employed, such as at Blairgowrie, where crowds came from Dundee... A special squad of girl pickers always pulled rasps for punnets, as older women did not pick so quick and inclined to bruise the berries, more, so they always, with children, picked into pails, small one, carried, tied with cord round waist, and large set at end of drill to be filled from small one.'

Geordie Watt, who picked raspberries as a boy in the 1920s near Auchterarder in Perthshire, wrote a song about it. The chorus goes:

Ye tak yer ain dreel
And then yer twa pails
Then fill them baith up
And awa tae the scales
At a hapny a pun [pound]
Ye've tae pu' near a ton
Tae mak a day's pay
At the berries.

A happy group of herring gutters, packers and coopers in the 1920s. The women - the gutters and packers - are from Lewis; the men either from Lewis also or from ports along the east coast. The location of the photograph is not known but may well be where the herring season ended in one of the English ports of Scarborough, Great Yarmouth or Lowestoft. The young woman in the front row is holding *cleeks*, hooks used to help lift the barrels.

HARVESTING THE SEA

Fishing has always represented a potential source of food and income for communities living by the sea. However, until well into the 18th century fishing was pursued only on a very small scale in most parts of Scotland. In the autumn and winter crofter-fishermen used baited lines to fish for white fish such as haddock, cod and ling. In summer, drift-nets were used to catch the migrating shoals of fish which swim near the surface, such as herring and mackerel. With the difficulty in preserving the fish and getting it to markets quickly, it provided only additional food and some extra income for essentially agriculture-based communities. Only in the enclosed waters of the Clyde estuary did the herring drift-net fishery, aided by the proximity of Glasgow markets, represent a significant, large-scale enterprise.

By the early 19th century, the situation had improved. Government interest and investment in the fisheries increased. Fishing villages and curing stations were set up, Macduff and the Pulteneytown District of Wick, the latter erected in 1808, and Ullapool and Tobermory in the west. The Dutch method of curing was adopted and renamed the 'Scotch Cure'. Later, as the railways developed and boats became decked and larger in size, fishermen were able to sail further afield, exploit new fishing grounds and, on their return, reach their markets more rapidly.

The great boom in the Scottish fishing industry came between the 1880s and the First World War. It was centred on herring and supplied mostly foreign markets with cured fish. The principal fishing fleets were based in Orkney, Shetland and all the way down the east coast. The season opened in late May when the herring appeared off the Western Isles. The boats followed the shoals around the north of Scotland and down the east coast, until the Scottish season finished in September. For the larger boats fishing continued into English waters, finishing in the East Anglian ports in early December. The winter was spent refitting in home ports and engaged in the non-seasonal fishing for white fish.

The labour force necessary to process the vast herring catches was recruited at the beginning of the season, either locally or from sea-based communities all around the coasts. In particular, the workers came in huge numbers from the Western Isles. Large numbers of men, women and girls employed as gutters, packers, coopers and curers followed the fleets either on the boats themselves or using the railways to go from port to port. The herring industry suffered badly during the First World War, recovered between the wars, but little remained of it after the Second World War. We are very fortunate that developments in photography occured in time to record the Scottish herring fishing boom from its beginnings.

Although almost certainly posed, this photograph shows many of the methods and implements used in the autumn and winter white fishing, mainly for haddock and cod, in Auchmithie, Angus, around the 1890s.

The woman seated at the right is shelling mussels for bait. The fisherman is pausing in the process of *redding* his lines - checking them for damage and removing any old bait and other debris. And the neat woman in the centre is taking the prepared line from the basket at her feet, baiting its hooks and laying it very carefully in the basket at her right, with alternate layers of grass and hooks to prevent the hooks from snagging each other, ready for the next fishing trip.

The cleaning, baiting and preparation of the lines could take up to ten hours and was therefore very much a family effort. Amongst the array of objects in this photograph are several of the long, low line baskets or *sculls* used to hold the fishing lines and from which they were cast out from the boats.

J B White, Dundee

In 1937, aged 83, Mrs Betsy Jack was still shelling mussels to be used as bait for the fishing lines. She is working, seated in the net shed opposite her cottage in Avoch on the Black Isle. A wooden board over the tub or *sae* of unshelled mussels holds dishes of mussels and a basin of water into which the shelled mussels are placed in order to clean them. With two to three mussels per hook and lines of 500 to 1,500 hooks, the job of shelling was enormous and time-consuming.

Fishing nets and cork floats are stored on the high shelf behind Mrs Jack, and a row of fishermen's socks hangs drying below them.

Fife fishermen preparing their fishing gear at St Monance for a new season of herring fishing in about 1905. Although posed, this photograph shows an interesting display of fishing equipment: waterproof oilskins and sou'westers, fishermen's leather boots and several nets with small cork floats. The two large circular objects are metal *pallets*, floats used to keep each net at the correct depth. The fishermen themselves are wearing heavy everyday-wear leather boots, tweed trousers and the wool *gansey* jerseys common to most fishing communities.
William Easton, St Monance

St Monance herring fishermen preparing their nets aboard their boat moored in the harbour, about 1900. Urgent repairs are being carried out and the nets untangled and sorted, ready for the next fishing trip.
William Easton, St Monance

Fisherman J Buttars getting a hair-cut or brush from a 'barber' aboard his boat moored at the East Pier in St Monance harbour, in about 1910. Although obviously posing for local photographer William Easton, all four fishermen seem highly amused. To the right of the men is a Beccles steam capstan, used for hauling the nets and hoisting the sails, a recent innovation which eased the hard physical labour needed on a fishing boat.
William Easton, St Monance

Lifting a heavy two-handled quarter cran basket holding roughly 200 herring, possibly at Ullapool, in the 1950s. (A cran is a volume measure of herring, representing about 750 fish.)

Both the men and the quay are liberally spangled with glittering fish scales. By the 1950s fishermen's clothes had lost a lot of their individuality - factory-made cotton dungarees and plain woollen jerseys replaced the tweed trousers and elaborately-knitted ganseys.

David Innes, Currie

The Inverness-registered steam drifter *Mistress Isa*, with other steam drifters in the background. This photograph, taken around the 1920s, shows a wooden boat. Introduced in the final years of the 19th century, steam drifters slowly replaced sailing boats and were themselves supplanted by motor-powered boats during the 1920s and 1930s.

Although powered by steam, these drifters, as the photograph shows, were also provided with sails. The foremast on this boat has been lowered where several men are working. Further back piles of nets and floats can be seen; and in the stern oilskins hang over the lifeboat.

Skate being hauled onto the pier with the help of a gaff at Stornoway, Lewis, in about 1906, much to the interest of the onlookers. The fishermen are wearing leather sea-boots over their tweed trousers, and thick woollen jerseys. Herring barrels are in the background. Skate, like other white fish, were caught with lines and hooks rather than nets. They were sold fresh locally or were wind-dried and shipped elsewhere.

A fishing net being hoisted up the mast to help disentangle it and sort out the fish, in St Monance harbour, about 1900. The scene seems to be of great interest to the two well-dressed boys in their Eton collars sitting on the bollard, and to the more informally-dressed group on the right.
William Easton, St Monance

Steam trawlers moored in the harbour at Aberdeen in the early 1900s. Unlike other types of fishing, steam trawling tended to be concentrated in a small number of large ports, of which Aberdeen was the principal one in Scotland. It differed also in that boats were company-owned, rather than owned by their skippers or skipper and crew together.

Loch Fyne ring-net fishermen hauling in their net in the early 1900s. The ring-net evolved from the drift-net in the early 19th century. It hung down in the water and was used to encircle herring shoals, as here, in enclosed waters. Usually two boats worked together, the first holding one end of the net while the other towed the net round in a huge circle.

Campbeltown-registered Loch Fyne skiffs, used by ring-net fishermen, tied up at the pier in Campbeltown, probably over a weekend, in about 1905. The rope spread out to dry on 54CN is almost certainly a sweepline, used to haul ring-nets from deep water into shallow water. Engines did not begin to be introduced onto these boats until 1907.
Charles MacGrory, Campbeltown

Campbeltown fishermen mending
their herring nets on the new quay
between about 1890 and 1910. Nets
were expensive and had to be maintained in excellent condition to
make sure that they would last for as
long as possible. A neglected or
badly-repaired net disintegrated very
rapidly.
Charles MacGrory, Campbeltown

The Montrose-registered Fifie *Trustful* of Gourdon, Kincardineshire, in her home port. Fifies, distinguished by their vertical stem and stern, took their name from the county in which they were first built and used in the late 19th century. They were usually painted black with a little white at the bow.

This one was built in about 1911 and was still very much a working boat when this photograph was taken in the autumn of 1974. She was one of the first Fifies built with both sails and a motor engine. Many were converted from sail to motor engines in the 1930s and 1950s. The hatches could be removed to allow room for rowing if required.

She has just returned from a fishing trip: the lines are lying in untidy piles, with unused bait and other debris still attached to them. Fishermen's protective clothing has changed since the beginning of the century - bright yellow oilskins have replaced their black predecessors and sea-boots are of rubber rather than leather.

Bruce Walker

The motor trawler *Iona* from Ness on the island of Lewis, in the 1960s or 1970s. The first steam trawlers appeared in the 1880s and for a time seemed to threaten the livelihoods of inshore fishermen. Their huge bag-shaped nets dragged along the sea-bottom and captured all the white fish in their path, leaving very little behind. Large-scale trawling is partly responsible for the over-fishing of the seas around Scotland. Today, trawlers of modest size make up most of the Scottish fishing fleet.

On the day this photograph was taken, the boat was being used not to fish but to ferry gannet hunters to the island of Sula Sgeir.

A good catch of white fish, cod, halibut and ling, laid out on the quay ready for auction, at Stornoway in Lewis, in about 1906. The proceeds of the auction would be divided up between the fishermen, according to the number of shares each had in their boat, and after clearing expenses. The Lewis Coffee House in the background was a favourite place for the fishermen.

Fisher-girls from the island of Barra, photographed during a pause in their work as gutters and packers at Ullapool quay, in 1929. Their fingers are bandaged to protect them from the effects of very sharp knives and salt, and both aprons and hands are covered in a mixture of salt and fish scales.

Women worked in teams of three or five, usually two gutters to one packer, and sometimes two acting as carriers and suppliers of salt. In the case of a three-woman team, the male coopers fetched and carried salt and barrels. As the processing had to be completed as quickly as possible, the women regularly worked twelve or more hours a day. Experienced gutters dealt with between 30 and 50 fish a minute.

Herring packers at work on the quay in the Fishmarket, Aberdeen, in 1903. A supply of gutted herring ready for packing is being brought over in a basket by two women, one of whom is also carrying a dish of salt balanced on her right hip. The three women knitting as they walk may be having a break. The balls of wool are pinned to their aprons and their needles probably supported by leather knitting belts or wooden knitting sheaths tucked into their waistbands. The three interested onlookers are well-dressed but without shoes - perhaps abandoned during a paddling expedition, or simply not worn at all to save wear.

A group of fisher-girls, almost certainly from Lewis, photographed in Fraserburgh, in about 1922. The four women in the centre of the front row are: Mary Macdonald, Catriona Macdonald, Iseabail Macdonald and Annie Macdonald. Kate Macleod is at the extreme left of the row. The others so far have not been identified.

In 1913, out of 12,000 Scottish women gutters, 5,000 went south for the English season, and of those 3,500 had set out from the Western Isles. As late as 1936, there were still almost 1,000 fisher-girls from the Western Isles amongst the 2,600 which followed the boats to East Anglia.

Iain Iain Bhàin, fish curer, standing outside a curing station on the shore of Loch Carloway, on the north-west coast of the island of Lewis, probably around the 1920s. By the time this photograph was taken the curing industry in Lewis, once famous for its salmon and ling, had all but disappeared.
Alasdair Alpin MacGregor

Possibly Tom Scott, photographed in about 1902 on the island of Foula, Shetland, in the process of building up or rebuilding a stack or *steeple* of dried cod or ling. This was the final stage of a complicated curing process which took about three months during which the fish were cleaned, salted, rinsed, drained and finally dried by sun and wind. The drying process was performed by alternately laying the fish out singly and building them into small heaps or *clamps* of ever-increasing size. Finally, a large steeple was built, periodically taken down and rebuilt in order to vary the position of each fish and thus achieve a uniform cure. When judged ready, the fish were either shipped immediately to mainland markets or stored in a dry wood-lined cellar for shipping later on and for local consumption. The mats which can be seen lying next to the steeple were probably used to protect it from the rain.

The Shetland *haaf* or open-sea fishing, of which this process was part, took place in sixereens - six-oared, open, undecked boats - which were rowed forty or fifty miles into the Atlantic to fish for cod and ling. The dangerous haaf fishing lasted until the 1880s when easier and safer means of fishing took over.

At work in a kippering house, possibly in Wick or Thurso, around 1900. This shows a stage in one of the many methods of curing or preserving fish. Herring are split open, washed, pickled in salt, then left to drip, and finally hung up to smoke in a kiln. The photograph shows herring being hung to drip on tenter sticks above the tentering trough in which they have been stirred around in brine for about twenty minutes. The tenter sticks are then placed in vertical rows in the kiln. The men keep the women supplied with fish and see to the smoking operation.

Pickled herring being canned for the American market at the Peterhead factory of Crosse and Blackwell in June 1958. Stainless steel has replaced the wood of the pickling trough in the earlier Caithness photograph, and cans have replaced barrels. The women's working conditions have also improved – the building is heated. Their hair is tied up in protective scarves in the fashion adopted during the Second World War.
Coopey of Aberdeen

Marianne Calder preparing oat meal bannocks in her home at Westside Cottage, Dunnet, Caithness in the autumn of 1969.

Mrs Calder went on to bake them in much the same way as described by Annie Stirling Stronach, speaking of early 20th-century Banffshire:

'The round (of dough) was shovelled gently off the board on to the girdle, fired, and cut in four quarters when it was just ready for turning. The quarters were turned by putting your hand on top and the knife in below an files ye burnt yer han an files ye broke yer breid. The other side was fired, then the quarters were set down in front of the fire to finish off - to make it more crisp and brown.'

NMS

AT HOME

The home is a centre of our lives, yet, because it is regarded as mundane and also private, it remains largely unrecorded. Traditionally, home life has been the main area of women's activity, and thus the huge contribution made by women's work in the home has been overlooked by the camera: the rearing of children, housework, food preparation, laundrywork, spinning, knitting and sewing, dairywork, poultry-keeping and the behind-the-scenes care of fishing equipment, rarely feature in photographs.

In 1970 Marianne Calder wrote of the life of a crofter's wife in Caithness and described what photographs cannot show us:

> After enjoying a morning cup of tea it's out to give the morning feed of oats to the poultry, then do the milking and feed the calf or calves... Surplus milk being put in basins the cream of which is kept and churned into butter once a week for household use, and if (there is) any surplus it can be sold to the grocer's van which calls once a week. The man of the house attends to the feeding of the cow or cows in the winter time. In the summer (he) turns them out to grass where they remain till about 7pm when milking time comes round again. After morning milking...housework has to be attended to...then breakfast has to be made... Then a panfull of potatoes are daily boiled and mixed with mash and fed to the poultry at mid-day.
>
> After a cup of tea or snack about one o'clock it is generally time to get dinner cooked and again about 4pm poultry has to get fed with oats, eggs collected and washed ready for the van to collect. Monday is generally washing day which is easily done now by washing machine, not so long ago a big pan had to go on the fire to boil water for the washing then clothes soaked and scrubbed on a washing board before being hung out to dry...
>
> Then baking is another of the housewife's chores which can now be done using the electric cooker, but is still being done on at least one croft...on a girdle hung on a crook above the peat fire...
>
> When outside work has to be done the crofter's wife generally lends a hand, such as at turnip thinning, threshing, coling hay, harvest work, potato lifting and also when peat cutting is in progress which generally takes place in May.

Many of the photographs included here were taken by staff of the National Museums in an attempt to fill the gap in the historical record. These photographs are the best of a small collection rather than the best of a large one. For the future, we should perhaps think of the importance of the work carried out within the home and record it.

Piece-time during the hay harvest at Pitglassie, near Auchterless, Aberdeenshire in the 1950s. Lizzie Cordiner has brought a drink out to the men. They are: Jim Hunter, Jim Cordiner, James Hunter and John Gall.
Alexander Fenton, NMS

Women helpers plucking chickens in preparation for the several hundred guests invited to an Eriskay wedding in 1960. The only container large enough to boil the chickens was a washing-boiler.
Kenneth Robertson, Stornoway

Will Strachan having his piece
during a break in the peat cutting on
Crombie Moss, Banffshire in the
summer of 1968.
Alexander Fenton, NMS

Christina MacKenzie limewashing her cottage at Cullipool on the island of Luing, Argyllshire, about 1950.

Limewashing, which is usually carried out once a year, is done partly for aesthetic reasons and partly to give the walls additional protection against the elements. Internal limewashing, as well as brightening the house, was used as a disinfectant.

Various substances, such as clays, can be added to the limewash to colour it if required.

Alasdair Alpin MacGregor

Daily chores at Gormyre Farm, near Torphichen, West Lothian, about 1900. One woman carries milk or water pails with the help of a wooden yoke, whilst the other sweeps the doorstep with short-handled brush and shovel. The two folded sacks may be to keep her boots from bringing dirt back into the house, and possibly to be used to kneel on when scrubbing the steps.

Thomas Comb, perhaps on his daily walk, looks on.

Thomas Comb and his wife Helen Whitelaw taking their porridge at Gormyre Farm about 1900.

A house interior at North Biggins on the island of Foula, Shetland, in 1902. Fishing lines, fishermen's knitwear and gutted and split fish of the cod family (possibly coalfish) hang drying above the fireplace. Note also the clay floor and the cruisie lamp (an open, boat-shaped lamp with a rush wick which often burned fish oil) hanging at the right of the fireplace. The rack hanging on the left was put over the fire so that cooking pots could be placed on it.
H B Curwen Collection

Mrs MacPhail in the kitchen-living room of her home at Locheport on North Uist, in the autumn of 1970.

The house, a development of the traditionally-built blackhouse, had a chimney at each gable and a third near the centre. The stone walls were about three feet thick and it was thatched with heather weighted with stones.
J R Baldwin, NMS

John and Maggie Anne Mouat in their home at Houbie on the island of Fetlar, Shetland, in August 1963.

Note the whitewashed hearth with the chimney built into the thickness of the gable wall, and the shelving, also built into the wall. The chain and pot hook above the highly polished grate are suspended from an iron bar or rantle-tree fixed across the chimney.
Alexander Fenton, NMS

Building partially-dried peats into rickles near Elrig village in Wigtownshire in 1959. The rickles expose the maximum surface of the peat to the air helping them to dry as fast as possible. They are then taken home to be stacked.

In areas without coal supplies, peat provided fuel for cooking and heating houses until gas and electricity arrived in the second half of the 20th century. Peats are still cut for fuel in some areas today.
Alexander Fenton, NMS

Doing two jobs at once. Doreen Murray demonstrating how she could bring home peats and knit at the same time, at Ness on Lewis, about the 1930s.

Iain Aonghais Choinneach, otherwise known as Spuigean, of Doune Carloway, Lewis, photographed in the early 1900s wearing a beautifully-made, and probably his best gansey. Usually knitted in dark blue wool by fishermen's wives, daughters and sweethearts, these jerseys with their distinctive patterns and two side-buttons on the collar were characteristic of fishermen's dress until the First World war.

They provided comfortable, warm and moderately waterproof clothing.

Working ganseys would not be as elaborate as this one, but on the finest and best the pattern might extend down onto the sleeves.

Wilma O'Hara at the village water
pump in Cullipool, on the island of
Luing, Argyllshire, about 1950.
   Luing was famous for its slate,
which was mostly used for roofing.
A pile of slate can be seen in the
background, and Wilma is standing
on a slate outcrop.
Alasdair Alpin MacGregor

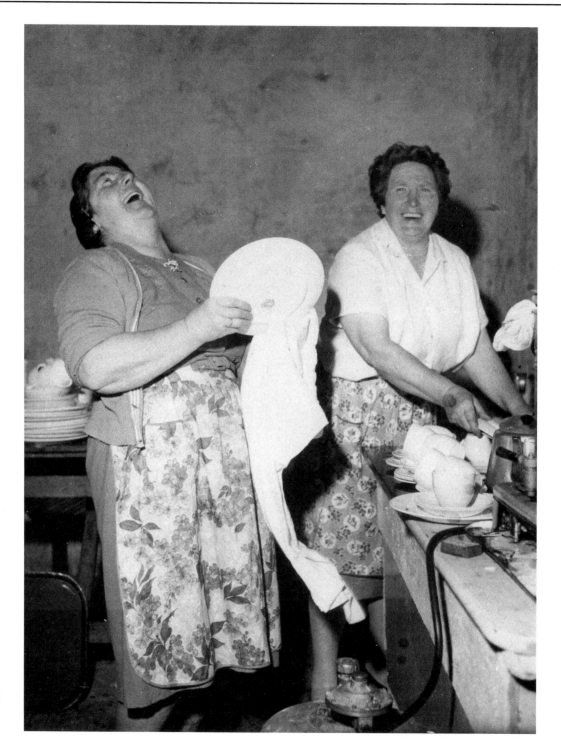

Dish-washing volunteers at an Eriskay wedding in 1960. On the day following the wedding, the helpers were rewarded by being invited to a meal at which bride and groom waited upon them.
Kenneth Robertson, Stornoway

Lucy Alison, washerwoman, at Burnside, St Monance, in the 1900s. She is at work outside, using a large wooden washing tub with a ringer clamped onto it. For centuries laundrywork has provided many women with additional income, or for those without other means of support, with their only income.
William Easton, St Monance

A gannet hunter from Ness, Lewis, plucking a guga (a young gannet) on the island of Sula Sgeir, north of the Butt of Lewis, in August 1954. After plucking, the birds are singed over a peat fire to help loosen the remaining feathers, gutted and finally salted to preserve them for up to several months. The singeing process also adds a slightly smoky taste to the flesh.

Today the Sula Sgeir gannet hunt is the last remaining, and the number of birds taken is strictly controlled, both by law and by the men themselves who have always known the stocks had to be maintained.

J McGeoch, Inverness

CRAFTS AND INDUSTRIES

Farming and fishing by themselves did not provide employment, goods and services for all in Scotland's countryside. Along with these major industries, others developed to service them and to process their products. Industries and crafts have also made use of the resources available in the countryside, such as water power for driving machinery; or stones, timber, grass, heather or rushes to provide building and road-surfacing materials and basic domestic equipment.

Blacksmith, joiner, cartwright and wheelwright were the backbone of the village economy, making and maintaining tools, implements, domestic equipment and means of transport. Since the middle of the 20th century, however, with the revolution in agriculture brought about by tractors and mass-produced, sophisticated machinery, there has been little traditional work for the blacksmith. But the few remaining horses still need shoeing, some agricultural machinery can be repaired without going back to the factory and there is work for those who have specialised in decorative wrought iron. Until iron became plentiful and cheap in the late 18th century, followed by other metal alloys and plastics in the 19th and 20th centuries, wood was vital for house timbers, tools and a multitude of domestic implements. Rural joiner, cartwright and wheelwright have all but disappeared also, their skills surviving mainly in the show carts and sporting gigs which are still made today.

In communities living in particularly harsh environments specific industries were developed. For the past four or five hundred years fowling for sea-birds, for instance, has been a vital part of their economies, providing additional food and oil and feathers which could be used or sold.

Some crafts, such as rope- or basket-making, developed as essential backups to the economy, providing goods for both domestic and agricultural use. Today home-made ropes have almost disappeared as commercially-manufactured ropes are now cheaply and easily available, and the very different nature of farming and house-building no longer requires them.

Other crafts, such as hand-knitting, are still practised today. From the early 17th century, hand-knitting became common throughout Scotland, providing households with warm and relatively waterproof garments and a product which could be sold or exchanged for other goods. As power-operated knitting machines became possible the domestic craft became an industry. The knitwear industry today is still an important part of the economy. Hand-knitting survives as a pastime, in the traditional specialised knitting of which Fair Isle patterns and Shetland shawls are examples, and in the craftwork revival of the 1970s and 1980s.

Happily plucking gugas at Port of Ness, Lewis, in the 1950s or 1960s. This may show one of the rare years in which bad weather forced the gannet hunters to bring back some of the birds unprocessed.

Traditionally, the journey to the bird colonies took place in open rowing, and later sailing, boats. It is only since the Second World War that the men of Ness have been able to go in motor boats for their annual expedition which takes about two weeks in good weather, longer if it is bad. The collecting of feathers for use as pillow-stuffing was abandoned earlier this century as the gannet odour is very difficult to get rid of.

Fishermen helping to haul a newly-built or repaired boat to the sea. In the background, another Fifie is nearing completion in St Monance boatyard, in the 1900s.

Until fishing declined dramatically in the 1940s and 1950s, most fishing communities built their own boats. Today, so few fishing boats are commissioned that boat builders have either gone out of business or have had to make desperate efforts to build and sell other types of boat, or raft such as oil platforms.
William Easton, St Monance

Boat-building at the yard of Smith and Hutton in Anstruther, Fife, in 1973. The men are fairing, or smoothing, out the boat's timbers with *eetches* (adzes) to ensure the planks they are about to nail into position lie flush. The yard has since closed.
Gavin Sprott, NMS

Bob (Bobbie) Robertson, honorary farrier to the Royal Highland Show, cold-shoeing Rab at Middle Norton Farm, Newbridge, Midlothian, in the 1970s.

The horse had a cracked hoof and a special shoe had been made to hold it in place. Horse-shoeing was only one of the many tasks which the village blacksmith performed for his community. The blacksmith made and repaired a wide range of agricultural implements and tools; made and fitted metal tyres and hub caps onto cart wheels and made cooking pots and other domestic utensils. He was a central figure in the rural community.

Ian Larner, NMS

John Guthrie, souter in Selkirk, photographed about 1972. Mr Guthrie retired in 1976 after 52 years in the trade. He was the last souter, or shoemaker, in Selkirk and the last of four generations of souters.

Until about the 1930s most country towns and villages had their own souters who made, as well as repaired, boots and shoes. Mechanisation has made the cost of completely hand-made footwear unviable for all but a few souters who either make shoes for the wealthy or specialise in a particular type of footwear. Dick Goudie, for instance, in Maybole, Ayrshire makes heavy boots for shepherds, farmers and gamekeepers.

Hand-made shoes today can cost £250. Mr Guthrie can remember making a pair for £2.10/-.

Preparing to ring a cart wheel at the Damacre Road Smiddy in Brechin, Angus, about 1910. Blacksmith Geordie Beattie, on the left, is measuring the circumference of an iron tyre using a traveller. The tyre had to be the exact circumference to fit the wheel for which it was intended. It was then heated until almost white hot and placed over the prepared wheel which was screwed down to the tyring platform, seen in the background. Water was then immediately thrown over the wheel to shrink the tyre into place and to stop the wheel from bursting into flames.

Note also the harrow presumably awaiting repair, leaning against the wall of the smiddy.

Mr Black, science master at Brechin High School.

Wheelwrights at work at Johnstone's Smiddy, East Pilton, Edinburgh in about 1912. Judging by the shades of the wood, they have been mending a damaged cart wheel and are in the process of fitting the last fillie (felloe) making the rim of the wheel.

Wheelwrighting is an extremely skilled craft because it relies entirely on pressure to keep the work together. Wheelwrights and blacksmiths worked closely together, and their workshops were consequently frequently adjacent to each other. The village wheelwright, more often than not the joiner and cartwright also, produced a wide range of tools and implements, domestic equipment and coffins.

A pattern shop at the Agricultural Implement Works of the firm of Alexander Jack & Sons, at Maybole, Ayrshire, about the 1880s. The firm was founded in 1852 at Maybole by Alexander Jack. He had trained as a joiner and cabinet-maker, had tried his hand unsuccessfully at farming, but his cartwrighting and agricultural implement factory prospered and came to be known worldwide. In 1905 the *Ayrshire Post* reported that the works were employing about 150 people.

The firm eventually closed down in the 1960s, its records being split between the Scottish Record Office which has the written records and the National Museums of Scotland which hold a large collection of photographs.

Repairing the lade at Finzean sawmill on the Water of Feugh in the forest of Birse, Aberdeenshire, in the late 1890s. The mill was established in the first half of the 19th century and relied on birch timber from the surrounding forest. The present owner, David Duncan, is the fourth generation of his family to operate the mill. His grandfather Alexander Duncan is seated holding an axe, and two of the small boys are his father David Duncan (1891-1977) and uncle George Duncan (1888-1976).

About a mile upstream, the Finzean Bucket Mill - the last in Scotland - has been restored with the help of the National Museums and is now a working turning mill. It is open to the public.

A team of timber workers, in Midlothian about 1920. The men probably including cutters and hauliers.

Cross-cut saws like the one shown here, operated by two men, were used until steam-driven felling equipment, and later chain saws, replaced them. The other basic tool is the axe used to cut branches and to start cutting a tree trunk before continuing with a saw. Note that the man on the left has wound sacking round his legs to protect them. He also has a rudimentary bandage on his right index finger. The only form of protective clothing visible here are the aprons worn by two of the men and the steel-capped boots worn by some of them.

Will Stormonth hiving (collecting) a
swarm of bees in Glen Esk, Angus,
in 1968. Note his straw bee skep, or
hive, and his protective gloves and
head covering. The swarm had just
been taken down from a tree branch.

Traditional skep beekeeping
relied on the bees' natural ability to
increase their numbers to the point
that a swarm of bees would split off
from the main colony to form a
new one. The swarms came off the
stock colonies in late May or early
June, were captured and put into
empty skeps.

When the flow of nectar
decreased in the autumn, the best
colonies were set aside and kept in
their skeps over the winter to
provide the next season's swarms.
The remaining skeps were placed
over sulphurous fumes in order to
kill the bees and extract the honey.
Alexander Fenton, NMS

In 1898 Andrew Carnegie purchased Skibo Castle, near Dornoch, as a summer residence. Major alterations were begun in 1899. Many of the local crofters, most of whom also had a trade, were employed on the building work. J L Goskirk's great uncles Donald and Robert Leslie worked on the site - Donald as a carter and Robert as a carpenter.

In order to get to work in time they left their home at Badninish, about six or seven miles from Skibo, at four o'clock each morning. This photograph, in which they have unfortunately not been identified, shows the workforce of carters, masons, joiners and site managers in front of the almost completed west wing.

The staff of Macallan's Whisky Distillery at Craigellachie in Banffshire in 1917. As fewer men were available because of the war, women and boys were employed. J Rugg, second left in the back row, was fifteen at the time and employed as the odd job boy. The man standing at the right is the exciseman and the cooper is seated on a barrel nearby.

The malt shovels are used to handle the barley from which whisky is made, especially for turning it during the malting and drying processes. They have been included in the photograph to act as symbols of the workers' occupation.

The hydro-electric power station for Stanley Cotton Mills, Perthshire, under construction in 1921. The man standing on the ladder is Sandy Robertson, foreman of the labourers. Behind him are Willie and John Culbert, interested twins who lived near the site.

Before the power station, the mills had been driven successively by a series of water wheels and a Gilkes turbine engine. In 1921 the lade was diverted to the new power station.

After the power station ceased to operate, a weir which diverted water from the River Tay into the lade was blown up in order to allow salmon to swim upstream more easily.

Stanley Mills and the adjoining village were established in the late 18th century. Spinning cotton at first, the mills converted to synthetic fibres during the 20th century. Growing foreign competition made them increasingly unviable and they finally closed in 1989.

A boy leading a garron (a small sturdy horse) laden with bundles of hand-cut reeds to be used for thatching buildings in the Errol area of Perthshire in 1940.

Various other materials such as heather, bent grass and straw have been used throughout Scotland for thatching; depending on what was available locally. In Perthshire the Tay reed-beds provided ample thatching material; and more recently have provided reeds for export to English thatchers. Today *Cairdean nan Taighean Tugha* (the Friends of the Thatched Houses society) provides practical and financial assistance and advice on the care of the few remaining thatched buildings in Scotland. It also maintains an extensive archive covering the whole country.

The maintenance of the dry-stone dykes which mark out field boundaries and help manage stock is an important job. A neat dyke also shows the countryside is cared for.

Skilled craftsmen are required to build good dykes. This is Tom Arres, on the left, repairing a dyke with his squad near Jedburgh in about 1970. Note the frame, the string and the four-pound hammer. These, with a foot rule, are the basic tools which have been used over the past two hundred years.
NMS

James Hunter and his son, also James, making an *edderin,* used to rope down stacks, at Brownhill Farm, Auchterless, Aberdeenshire, in 1959. They first made a rope of straw using the rope-twister or *thrawcrook,* the hooked end of which can just be seen held by James jnr. The loose end of the rope was then bent back and twisted under itself. Bending and twisting continued, and at each end of the growing edderin, the thrawcrook was given a half twist, to help spiral the lengths into place. *Alexander Fenton, NMS*

Mrs Morrison of Rodel, in Harris, cleaning and processing shorn woollen fleeces in 1939. The washed fleeces are placed over a fence to dry.
Angus M MacDonald, ARPS

Once the fleeces are dry, the wool is carded with a pair of cards made of wooden boards, one side of which is covered in leather through which fine wire teeth protrude to do the carding. A handful of wool is taken from the fleece and worked between the cards in order to tease it out into a fine web of intermingled fibres, ready for spinning.
Angus M MacDonald, ARPS

Scraping crotal into buckets on Roineabhal, north of Rodel on Harris, in 1939. Crotal is one of the substances used to dye wool. Of the 40 different species of this lichen, about seven are most commonly used to produce a wide range of colours.

According to Margaret Fay Shaw Campbell in her book *Folk Songs and Folk Lore of South Uist*, crotal was gathered in the late summer and sun-dried. Alternating layers of crotal and wool were then placed in a pot, with water, and cooked until the required colour was obtained.

Nowadays wool is mostly cleaned, dyed and spun in factories in Lewis. The spun warp and weft yarns are then delivered to the homes of the Harris Tweed weavers in Lewis and Harris. After weaving, the cloth returns to the factory for the finishing processes. A small number of weavers, however, are still washing, dyeing and spinning at home to produce a highly sought-after tweed.
Angus M MacDonald, ARPS

Jessie Cattanach of Whigginton, Tarfside, Glen Esk, Angus, demonstrating the use of her muckle wheel to spin wool, in about 1910. Miss Cattanach, who lived to the age of 97, was the last person to use the muckle wheel in the glen. She spun the wool of the local blackface sheep and knitted stockings with it.

The muckle wheel was used in Europe from about the 13th century until well into the 19th century. A thread was spun from a bunch of yarn to the full stretch of the arm, or as here, a step or two back if the spinner was standing. The wheel was then stopped and turned in the opposite direction to wind the length of spun yarn onto the spindle, as the spinner walked forward.

Mrs Ann Sutherland and her niece Eloira spinning wool in the early 1930s to produce the very fine yarn needed to knit the open-work shawls for which Shetland is famous.

Mrs Sutherland is using a *Spinnie*, a small upright spinning wheel which became popular in Shetland at the beginning of the 20th century. Recalling his childhood in Shetland, John H Johnson wrote about the wheels: 'the Spinnie was much more compact, lighter to operate, and did the job every bit as well as the earlier types of wheel. Also, it found immediate favour with the young women who went out to *Spinneens* [spinning gatherings]...'
Scotsman Picture Calendar, 1936

Mrs Helen Stout of the township of Busta, on Fair Isle, Shetland, knitting one of the jumpers for which the island is famous, about the 1950s. Fair Isle patterns for caps, scarfs and socks are mentioned in travellers' accounts dating from the early 19th century, but it was not until the Prince of Wales wore a Fair Isle jersey while golfing at St Andrews in 1922 that Fair Isle styles became very popular.
Alasdair Alpin MacGregor

Maggie Macdonald, of Arisaig,
bringing home bracken to be used as
bedding for cattle, in the early 1900s.
She is using a length of rope, twisted
around her hand to help spread the
weight of the load.

TRADE AND TRANSPORT

Getting to the shops is still not easy today in some parts of Scotland. The movement of people, goods and stock has been both helped and hindered by Scotland's topography: hills, rivers and the sea can be formidable barriers or used to facilitate transport. Bridges and ferry crossings were well established by the late middle ages, and boats were used extensively both on rivers and around the coast as they could move large loads relatively easily and cheaply.

Before the farming improvements of the 18th century, there were few roads in Scotland. Travellers used simple, well-known routes, drove-roads, paths and tracks. There was little stimulus to develop metalled roads, especially in the more remote areas, as wheeled vehicles were uncommon. Most things were moved on the human back or by packhorses, and beasts moved themselves. These were still important methods of transport in some areas until at least the middle of the 20th century.

From the 1850s, railways became a regular feature of the mainland countryside. The Strathmore line in Angus, for instance, had thirteen branches to small towns in a mainly agricultural area. As the railway advanced, from the 1880s onwards, places such as Kyle of Lochalsh and Mallaig became busy fish-curing centres, increasingly dependent on rail as well as coastal transport. Contraction of the railways started in the 1930s, when lorries and buses began to have a real impact. Today the car has taken over, arguably not always to the advantage of all those living in the countryside.

The development of improved transport and communications throughout the 19th century steadily eroded the need for the once-essential fairs, the only opportunities people had to gather together to buy and sell goods, stock and agricultural produce. Roups, or auctions, catered for the sale of beasts and implements, and from the 1880s, cattle marts in the small towns became increasingly common. Village shops grew up with good lines of supply to and from the towns.

The two following passages give some insight into life in two very different parts of Scotland in the early years of this century. The first, by Lady Maitland of Reswallie, describes trading in rural Angus: 'The 'pig-wife' came round quite often. She had a flat cart and a pony. The cart was full of china, known as pig... She exchanged her bits of china for rabbit skins, feathers and rags.' This next passage, by Marianne J Calder, a crofter's wife, describes a different venture in Caithness: 'Horse-drawn lorries and big carts used to come out from Thurso to our place in Reay 12 miles with loads of merchandise for the people from the neighbouring county of Sutherlandshire. They would all be down with their little carts and ponies to meet them, and take back the things.'

Shetland ponies being relieved of their loads of partly-dried peats on the shores of Moo Wick bay at the south-east tip of Lamb Hoga on Fetlar, Shetland in 1930.

The peats are neatly piled into stacks before being taken off the trackless peninsula by boat. The straw panniers or *cassies* holding the peats are slung from a wooden pack saddle placed over a straw mat. Rope nets around the panniers hold the peats in place. The men have just removed the net from one of the ponies and are unloading and stacking the peats.
J Gardner

A group of men and a boy, happily posing for the camera and helping to load sheep for transport by boat in Orkney in the 1920s or 1930s.

Leading home a Highland pony laden with dried peats carried in willow creels on a bright summer day on the island of Eigg in about 1905. When cut, peats are at least partially dried on site to make it easier to carry them home.
M E M Donaldson

The staff of Bankfoot station in Perthshire, standing in front of a Caledonian tank engine in 1916. They are: guard, William Innes, clerk, Andrew Graham, station master, Andrew Drew, engine cleaner, John Grant, fireman, J Dewar, parcel porter and gatekeeper, John Haggart, and engine driver, James Calum, holding an oil can.

The Bankfoot branch of the main Perth to Aberdeen line was opened to passenger traffic in 1906. Although passenger traffic was never heavy, this branch line, like those in many other parts of Scotland, was a vital link between the countryside and towns. Passenger traffic on this line stopped in 1931 through the pressure of competition from buses, but goods traffic continued until the line's closure in 1964.

Steam traction was used on roads as well as railways. This Foden Steam Wagon 'Busy Bee' was bought by A Craik, coal merchant in Alyth, in 1914 for carting stone. In 1922 John Doe, haulage contractor in Errol, purchased it. Its top speed was about seven miles per hour. This photograph, taken in 1926 at the top of Glamis Road, Dundee, shows it hauling wood from Kinnoul Hill outside Perth. The men are David Easson, driver, and A Wilkie.

Bringing the peats home to Ness on
Lewis, in the 1950s. On 'lorry day'
neighbours gathered to help each
other bring home their winter
supply of peats. Peat transport by
lorry ended in Ness about 1960.
Since then tractors have transported
peats straight from the peat banks to
people's homes.

Retired Grangemouth banker Selby MacKay with his wife, and the Misses Duncan seated in the back of his brand new Rover Landaulette, photographed in the Dunoon area in 1908. The first cars appeared in Scotland in the mid-1890s. In 1908 they were still a luxury which only the wealthy and some businesses could afford. Even when enclosed, early cars had no heating, and the driving gloves, blanket, fur collars and muff were necessary on cold days.

The Kinross County Council Invicta steam roller and its crew surfacing the road between Scotlandwell and Kinnesswood (now the A911), photographed between about 1915 and 1920.

John Gardiner, roadman, at work
with his scythe on a Lanarkshire
roadside in 1980.
Hugh Cheape, NMS

Mr Hay, driver and delivery man for Forbes Simmers, baker at Hatton and Cruden Bay, Aberdeenshire, photographed with the firm's travelling van – a Model T Ford – in the early 1920s. For dispersed rural communities, travelling shops provided an essential service as they continue to do today. Simmers' 'famed oatcakes and butter biscuits' are still well-known.

A trap being used as a milk van at Cotton of Kingennie in Angus in about 1900. Until the Milk Marketing Boards took over milk distribution in 1933, farms sold their milk directly to housewives who brought their milk containers out to the van to be filled up. Usually twice a day, after milking, the van would drive around villages selling milk. The milkman is wearing a leather pouch, with the strap across his shoulders, to hold money and a note-book recording milk sold, and amounts owed to him. The oil lantern attached to the front of the cart provided some light in the early morning and on winter evenings.
W M Brown, Dundee

Phemie, a fishwife, selling fish to Mrs Walker in the village of Corstorphine outside Edinburgh in the early 1900s. Phemie, dressed in the costume typical of fishwives from this part of the east coast, would have taken a No 12 tram up from Musselburgh or Newhaven with her willow basket and creel and wooden gutting board placed on the platform next to the driver. The letter F on the creel is thought to be the initial of the alternative spelling of Phemie.

John Donald, baker in Portsoy, Banffshire, serving a customer from his travelling van, in the village of Cornhill in 1974.
Alexander Fenton, NMS

The staff, family and premises of D Y Walker, butcher, on the corner of Millgate Loan and West Grimsby Street, Arbroath, in about 1915. They are: Grace Walker, D Y Walker, the clerkess, D Y Walker jnr, the butcher and the message boy. D Y Walker jnr took over the running of the shop in about 1920, aged only fifteen, on his father's death. By the time he sold the business in the early 1950s, he had two other shops and three vans serving the countryside around Arbroath, each van being on the road six days a week. Specialities appear to be corned beef and pickled tongues.

Eriskay women carrying home
heavy sacks of flour just put ashore
for them among the rocks from a
small boat, about 1947. The woman
on the left has wrapped a piece of
old cloth around her shoulders to
help ease the chafing of the sack, and
possibly also to protect her clothes.
A thatched island house can be seen
peeping over the brow of the hill –
home of one of them, perhaps.
Alasdair Alpin MacGregor

Neil Ferguson, the island post-master's son, carrying the last sack of St Kilda wool plucked from the famous local sheep to the jetty ready for shipment on the eve of the island's evacuation in August 1930.

Although not unduly heavy, the stoop of Neil Ferguson's back shows that the bulky load was awkward to carry.
Alasdair Alpin MacGregor

The afternoon plane – a de Havilland Dragon Rapide – from British European Airways' airport at Renfrew, just landed on the beach of Tràigh Mhór at the northern end of the island of Barra in about 1946-47. The vital daily Loganair flights linking the island to the mainland still land on this beach today. The Air Ambulance service serving the Highlands and Islands was instituted in 1934 by John Sword, director of Midland and Scottish Air Ferries Ltd. In April 1973, Loganair took over the Scottish Air Ambulance contract from BEA.
Alasdair Alpin MacGregor

Perhaps because of the very special-
ized nature of the skills required in
fishing and the ever-present danger,
fishing communities have tended to
be unusually close-knit. This close-
ness has perpetuated a multitude of
beliefs and traditions. Here in the
grounds of Pinkie House in 1948,
Musselburgh fishwives are dancing
during the annual Fishermen's Walk
celebrations, traditionally held at the
beginning of September to mark the
end of the summer fishing season.
Originally created as a friendly
society, the Musselburgh
Fishermen's Walk Society provided
help and pensions to the fishermen
and their families in Fisherrow. In
1912 the society had to dissolve as
fewer were involved in the fishing
or able to pay their contributions. In
1930, however, the Society was
revived by Alex Craig, and since
then the annual Fishermen's Walk
has been preserved.
C & F McKean

COMMUNITY

Community life and personal life are bounded by organisations, events and people which give them a structure. In our personal lives, birth, marriage, anniversaries and death are milestones which we share with relatives and friends. The first three are also likely to be the most photographed events in our lives, while funerals, except for those of the rich and famous, are very rarely recorded.

Community life relies on many people and a complex infrastructure, providing, for instance, a water supply, lighting, street cleaning, sewage disposal, a means of exchanging news, medical care and transport. Again these tend not to be recorded except where they can be personalised or made into an event. Photographs of characters of particular importance to a community, such as the town crier, are fairly common. Similarly civic events such as the turning on of domestic water supplies or electric street lighting will be recorded.

As well as existing for our spiritual needs, churches provide practical help in times of need and also help to maintain traditions and patterns of behaviour. We do not make photographic records of ourselves in church, except at christenings and weddings; but we do record Sunday School outings or striking events in the church's history - the laying of the first stone of the new building or the purchase of new Communion plate.

Belonging to sub-groups within a community is also part of our lives and group occasions will be photographed. Friendly societies for instance, like churches, provided help in the days before a national health service or state-run social security. Equally, belonging to a particular workforce, school group or sports club, helps to define an individual's identity within their community; and photographs provide proof of that identity and may well help to reinforce it.

Wartime has been an important part of the lives of people born between about 1880 and 1940 and many families and communities have recorded this through the thousands of formal photographs of uniformed young people or military processions.

This photograph shows that part of the Free Church congregation in Lochcarron, Ross-shire which split off to form the United Free Church in 1905. Excluded from using the parent church building, they held services outdoors until they constructed a temporary church to provide shelter. A permanent building was constructed in 1909-10 and is now the Church of Scotland West Church.
Dr C G Mackay, Medical Officer for Lochcarron from 1873 to 1917

A Sunday School outing taking refuge in the straw barn of Carvenom Farm near Anstruther, photographed between about 1905 and 1908.

The party were set to go on a corn cart to the beach at Elie but the weather turned very wet on the day. All are wearing their best summer clothes and their faces reflect a mixture of anxiety at being photographed, disappointment at the rain and the loss of Elie beach and, in a very few, pure enjoyment of a day out.

Four generations of the same family. This christening photograph, taken in Errol, Perthshire, about 1910, probably shows baby with mother, grandmother and great-grandmother. The eldest is Kate Robertson.

The Bride's Cog at an Orkney wedding in the 1950s. Traditionally the Bride's Cog, containing hot ale, whisky, beaten eggs and sugar, was circulated at the end of the wedding festivities. The tradition continues today, although the timing of the cog's arrival is now less important. *William Hourston, Stromness*

Mr and Mrs Andrew Birse celebrating their Golden Wedding in Glen Esk, Angus in 1898. After the wedding itself, the celebrations marking the major anniversaries of the event are some of the most frequently photographed milestones in our lives, providing a sense of continuity and stability.

Domhnull Iain Dhomhnuill Mhoir
(Donald Macarthur) schoolmaster, of
21 Knock on the Eye peninsula in
Lewis, photographed with his wife
on their wedding day in 1935. She is
wearing a beautiful satin wedding
dress and shoes.
Whyte of Inverness

The Jaffrey family in front of their croft at Hatton of Ardoyne, near Oyne in Aberdeenshire in about 1900. They are, standing: John, Leslie, Mary his wife, Leslie jnr and seated, John, his grandson – also John – and wife Sara Stewart Jaffrey.

The two elder Johns – father and son – were thatchers. Some of their tools are now in the National Museums' collections.

The thatch is a mixture of straw and clay. The wooden bars pinned across it to hold it in place are called rances. Note the ropework around the chimney of the adjoining building.

Children and passers-by watching fascinated as a water-barrel is filled at Cadger's Brig, Biggar, Lanarkshire, about 1900. The rolled-up trousers of some of the boys seem to indicate that either the water-cart or the photographer interrupted their play in the burn.

Water carts were used to collect drinking water and water to be used to damp down the dust in the streets.
Charles Reid of Wishaw

Margaret Cairns, district nurse, about to set off on her rounds on Fair Isle, Shetland in 1956: another important person in the rural community.
Alasdair Alpin MacGregor.

Donald MacRitchie, nicknamed Peedil, postman at Ness, Lewis, about the 1930s. Even since the arrival of the telephone, postmen and women have remained very important people in rural communities, taking letters and parcels to and from friends, relatives and mail-order companies and being the bearers of much interesting and important local news.

In the days before good roads and postal vans, many walked or rode - on pony or bicycle - several thousand miles a year.

A postal worker, possibly in Ratho, Midlothian, in 1916. During the First World War, in order to replace the men who had volunteered or been called up, many women were given jobs which were traditionally male occupations. For many women this was their first opportunity to be independent and their discovery that they could do 'men's work'.

The original of this photograph was printed as a postcard. The reverse reads: 'My dear Brother David, this is a photo of your postie sister... from your loving sister Mary.'

P Aitken, the Bellman of Newburgh, Fife, photographed in his best clothes in the early 1900s.

Before the telephones and when many people would not have been able to read local newspapers, the bellman or town crier had an important part to play in distributing local news: funeral notices were spread by the bellman, he might also advertise local cinema features and he could be commissioned to advertise any item of news. Many also lit the gaslights, emptied dustbins or rang the church bells, in effect acting as the village odd-job man.
Robertson

A provincial meeting of Freemasons at the masonic lodge at Tarfside, Glen Esk, Angus, in the 1900s.

Tom Duncan and Adam Simpson at a ploughing match at St Martins, Perth, in the 1930s or 1940s. The horses are in show harness and many hours of work will have gone into its preparation to compete for the prize of 'best pair'.

Ploughing matches were instituted at the end of the 18th century by agricultural societies as a means of spreading information on ploughing techniques and plough types, and of fostering pride in good work. They gradually declined as the tractor replaced the horse, but still take place as trials of skill for tractormen and as a means of testing plough types.

James Harrison, shoemaker, making two of the ba's for the traditional Christmas and New Year's Day ba games in Kirkwall, Orkney in 1947.

The Kirkwall Ba is one of a number of New Year's Day mass football games. Most of the others take place in the Borders. In Kirkwall, both men's and boys' games are played on Christmas and New Year's Day. The two teams of Up-the-gates (Uppies) and Down-the-gates (Doonies) are split according to place of residence at birth in relation to a line running east to west through Kirkwall town centre. Anyone can take part in the game, the object of which is to get the ball into the harbour for the Doonies, and up the street, to a fixed point, for the Uppies. The four leather ba's are made locally and at the end of the games are donated to the players judged to be the most worthy.
John D M Robertson

The ba is somewhere in the scrum of Uppies and Doonies in Victoria Street, Kirkwall, on New Years Day 1936.

On 28 December 1933 *The Orcadian* reported that: 'A sign of the times we live in appeared in the afternoon when a young woman actually retrieved the boys' ba' from the waters of the harbour. The rules of the game however were enforced with typical Victorian firmness and the lady surrendered the ball to a mere male. The incident suggests that it is perhaps time the Victorian rules of the contest were amended – if members of the fair sex are permitted to participate in the contest at all!' A ladies' ba was held in 1945 but was not a success and has so far not been repeated.

John D M Robertson

Men of the Royal Naval Reserve, photographed on Kirkwall pier, Orkney, during the First World War.

For centuries the lives of the people of Orkney have been intimately linked with the surrounding sea. The sea provided a living from the fishing and the experience which led many men either into service with the Navy or, from the 18th century, with the Hudson's Bay Company.

Scottish Women's Land Army girls in their distinctive dress uniforms of Canadian Mountie-type hats, overalls and jodhpurs. They are possibly taking part in a Harvest Festival parade at Muirkirk in Ayrshire, during the First World War.

The Women's Land Army was mobilised in the spring of 1917 to provide desperately needed farm workers to replace the thousands of men who had volunteered for the forces. This and other measures ensured that by the end of the war Britain was again able to feed herself without being too reliant on foreign imports.

Black Isle men of the Lovat Scouts at summer camp in Beauly, Inverness-shire in July 1914. This was a voluntary force who supplied their own horses in which they obviously took great pride.

The Lovat Scouts went on to fight in the Dardanelles at Gallipoli in the First World War.

The following rhyme was sung to an Angus correspondent by his grand-mother in about 1900. With the child's shoes off, one foot was knocked against the other, first the toes and then the heels:

John the Smith o fellow fine
Can you shoe this horse o' mine
Yes indeed and that I can
As weel as ony man
Pit a bit upon the tae
Tae gar the horsie climb the brae
Pit a bit upon the heel
Tae gar the horsie, pace weel
horse, pace weel

A completely natural portrait of a little girl photographed on a warm day, at Sanna, near the westernmost tip of Ardnamurchan, Argyllshire in about 1920. She may be the child of the photographer's neighbour.
M E M Donaldson

GROWING UP

For many of us, childhood is remembered as the happiest and most exciting time of our lives. This is in part because childhood is usually the time when we are at our fittest and healthiest, and in part because our memories tend to treasure the good things and forget the painful ones. But childhood is also the time when we are at our most inquisitive, exhilarated by learning and discovery, and free from many of the cares that come with adulthood.

Learning is formalised at school or Sunday school, but also takes place constantly through games, toys and play, both with other children and with adults, and in our delight in mimicking grown-up behaviour - usually encouraged and used by adults to teach us the social skills necessary to become independent and competent men and women.

Mabel Smith, a farm-worker's daughter in Aberdeenshire and herself a school-teacher, recalled her childhood and schooldays in the early 1900s:

> Toys were practically unknown to us. When at Mains of Slains, the farmer's widowed daughter...gave me a marvellously dressed doll with a wax face, which my sister promptly smashed. To comfort me, I suppose, somebody gave me a 'stick doll' which would no doubt have looked lovely had I not first seen the other...
>
> ...[when the schoolmaster was not feeling well and unwilling to use his voice] Invariably we would begin with [the] Bible, in which our ignorance always proved to be abysmal, infuriating the poor man, no doubt because at that time inspectors were sure to be keen on that subject. The strap was kept busy, till we were all terrified and then we would be set to do some written work and nobody would dare make any sound... We kept a cloot for cleaning our slates by the 'spit and rub' method, the boys sometimes using the sleeve of their jacket to give a final polish. The cloot soon smelt... When I first went to school we didn't have Christmas holidays. I'm told we had a day off at the New Year, a Term holiday, ie a week at the end of May, because there were so many cottars flitting then, and Hairst Play, which was six weeks at harvest time, when many of the bigger pupils had to help with the harvest... 'Sax weeks tae tear wir claes, an' ae day tae men' 'em' - always we had the 'ae day' the Monday off...

As the pictures shown here demonstrate, the photographs we take of children, generally recording them at their happiest, tend to reinforce our own memories of childhood. Nevertheless, they remain valuable records.

Another unidentified pair, probably brother and sister, sitting on a pier. The location of this photograph is unknown, the date about 1900. The tucks in the little girl's skirt allowed it to be lengthened as she grew. Note the home-carved wooden boat with its wallpaper sail.

Mabel Smith recalling other games wrote: 'I would play with pieces of coloured paper such as the wrapping of "Pinkie", used for cleaning spoons, the paper pink in colour, shiny and with a peculiar smell... One aunt used to "flipe" one of father's socks, turn it round so that the heel was supposed to be a doll's face, wrap a shawl round it and produce an old box to lay it in.'
Riddell Collection, Scottish Photography Archive

Playing bools (marbles) in 1956 under the fascinated gaze of a pet dog. The bools have different names according to their size, colour and the material they are made of: glessies, steelers, ruddies, limmies and roldies, for instance. There are also many different ways of playing. Here, the object of the game seems to be to flick the marbles into the hole.
T E Gray

Showing off a new bicycle, possibly at Blairlinn Farm on the site of Cumbernauld New Town, about the 1940s or 1950s.

Playing at being grown-up. A tea party, in 1954 at Congalton Gardens, near Drem in East Lothian. The children are June Sinclair, Thomas Middlemass, Ann and Bobby Sinclair. They haven't a miniature teaset, but have been provided with a very nice lace tablecloth and cake stand.

Children, clearly well-to-do, having a miniature tea party with a doll's teaset on 27 July 1903 in the Uists, Inverness-shire. The crockery and the stove, dresser and pots and pans are all perfect replicas of the adult versions. The cups also appear to contain real tea or cocoa (unless it's a mixture of mud and water).

Mabel Smith again: 'Later we played hoosies with broken crockery called "lames", also shoppies using small pebbles for money, sand for sugar, docken seeds for mince, scraped turnip for butter. Scraps of material were magnified into yards and so on. Schoolies of course were also played and every child wanted to be teacher and be able to use the strap.'
Cathcart Collection

Travelling people's children, possibly
encamped near Stromness in
Orkney, about the 1930s. Note the
hand-made wooden car at the feet of
the child on the left.
William Hourston, Stromness

Ian Graham of Edinburgh making friends with the local girls in Slamannan, Stirlingshire, in 1921. It would be fascinating to know what he and the eldest girl are doing. He was on a family visit to Margaret Taylor, who had worked for his family for over 60 years. Margaret, born in 1828 the daughter of the Slamannan blacksmith, had gone to Edinburgh in 1849 to care for Ian's great-great-grandfather. She then stayed on as nursemaid to the children of the family. She died in 1922.
Dr C W Graham, Edinburgh

Johanna MacDonald of the township of Skigersta in Ness, Lewis, bringing home water from a spring in the 1920s or 1930s. The hoop is used to relieve some of the pressure on the bearer's arms. It also helps to keep the splashing pail away from the body. All the water for the home and the animals was fetched in this way, in many places until as recently as the 1950s.

Fishing with home-made rods without reels in the Uists in the early 1900s – a game, but also a very useful skill.
Cathcart Collection

Ready to bring home the peats on the island of Barra, Inverness-shire, in the 1920s or 1930s.

Christina MacVarish bringing home firewood at Bracora, Morar, Inverness-shire in about 1905.

Christina was born in Bracora on 19 February 1898, the youngest of five children. Her father was drowned when she was two, leaving her mother alone to bring up their children on the croft. Aged twenty, Christina married Alexander MacDonald, head stalker on Meoble Estate on the other side of Loch Morar. They lived there for 36 years and had nine children. Alexander also died when his family were young, leaving Christina with five of them still at school. She died in 1986.

M E M Donaldson

Dressed in their best clothes, a class of Abernethy School at Nethy-bridge, Inverness-shire in about 1900. All the children's names are known although there is not enough space to list them here.

Some of them travelled up to six or seven miles to school.

Lamington Primary School, near Biggar, with teachers, in the 1930s. Mabel Smith recalled the games she played at school: 'We had ball games, when balls were not all burst and widna stot. Skipping had a long run. Beddies (hopscotch) were attempted, but the playground was rough and uneven... More than once we went to the sands at Cruden Bay for a school picnic. Parents and others came along too. We went by train, waving and shouting to any body or beast we saw on the way. People waved back and the horses bolted and capered. There were lots of kinds of races for pupils, and others for the grown-ups.'

Brian Stewart Wilson of the township of Schoolhouse on Fair Isle, Shetland, in 1956. Wearing his home-knitted Fair Isle jumper, he is bringing home a bunch of kail.
Alasdair Alpin MacGregor

Sizing up the game. John Lawler, chemist, photographed during a bonspiel (curling match) in Kinross-shire in the early 1900s. Note the besoms used to sweep the ice. Brushes are more common today.

'PLENTY ENTERTAINMENT'

Until the beginning of the 20th century paid holidays were unheard of for most people. Days off therefore were a rare treat and eagerly anticipated. For rural communities especially, the few holidays revolved around the days off for farm workers' hiring fairs granted twice a year, for the agricultural shows, and at New Year. The huge improvements in transport brought about by the railways allowed people to travel much further afield, and day trips to the seaside were particularly popular.

The 19th century, however, did see a huge increase in sporting activities. Greater emphasis was placed on the importance of sport to individual health and wellbeing, and various traditional sports such as football, golf and curling were organised and formalised through the creation of numerous sports clubs throughout the country.

Mabel Smith, whose father was a farm worker in Aberdeenshire, wrote of the entertainments available when she was a small girl in the early 1900s:

> We were lucky in having two unmarried uncles who always turned up at the 'terms'... Father and the uncles would play the melodeon turn about. Father might sing and the uncles recite. The men would smoke their pipes... There would be much laughing at jokes, then tea would be made... Nearly every farm servant could play the melodeon, many could also play the fiddle... There was a Flower Show at Auchmacoy... There were prizes for knitting, needlework, baking etc as well as for flowers and vegetables. In the open sports were held and there was a dancing board for competitions for adults and children. There might be a hat-trimming competition for the men...and maybe a nail driving competition for the ladies... The results caused much merriment, especially when the men donned their hats for the judging.

Marianne Calder wrote in 1970 of the entertainments available to crofters' wives in Caithness in the winter: 'During the winter months there's whist drives, church Women's Guild meetings, occasional concerts or social gatherings. WRI [Women's Rural Institute] meetings, and dances for the younger ones... Spare time can be taken up by knitting or sewing, and nowadays one can always get plenty entertainment on the Radio and Television.'

Photography has charted this rise in leisure time and sport but, as in many other fields, women are conspicuous by their absence. This is in part due to the fact that women have traditionally had far less leisure time than men, and partly because, until very recently, they have often been forced to adopt passive roles as onlookers rather than become participants in many sports.

Fishermen enjoying Amy McLean's ice-cream on a Saturday morning in early summer in Mallaig harbour, in the mid-1930s. Amy is making sliders, ice-cream wafers, using a small shallow metal box, known as a stamp. This type of confection took its name from the fact that once assembled, it was slid out of the stamp.

The men are Jock McIntyre and Sandy McKinlay from the *Kingfisher,* Archie Stewart and Malcolm McLean from the *Kingbird,* John Short Snr from *Nulli Secundus* and Charlie Durnin from *Blue Bird.*

The Burntisland Cricket Club team for the 1901 season. They are, standing in the back row: R Young, J Bell, P Simpson, Mitchell, J Mitchell, J D Boswell, Broadley, G A McAllister, Goodwillie (umpire); seated in the middle row: J Johnstone (captain), J J Kirke Esq (president), H Wilson, and D J B Kirk; seated at the front: J D Shaw (scorer), W Kinnell and D Connel.

Cricket was adopted from England and became very popular during the 19th century.

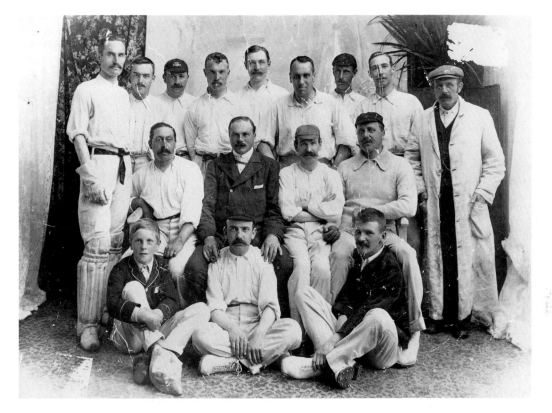

The Bishopshire Football Club of Kinnesswood, Kinross-shire in 1921.

Possibly a party of holidaymakers from the mainland sheltering from the rain in a bunker during a golfing holiday on the island of Islay, Argyll, in about 1892.

The boys were probably local, acting as caddies to make some money.

A stalking party in Morar, Inverness-shire, between 1872 and 1897. From the 1870s large deer forests were created on former mountain pastures, in response to the growing passion for deer stalking as a sport. The railways brought hordes of sportsmen to the Highlands every year, and large Scottish sporting estates provided at least seasonal employment for many country people, as stalkers, gillies, ponymen and domestic servants.

The trophies of a week's red deer stalking in Glenhurich Deer Forest in Sunart, Argyll, in 1960. Crouched in the foreground is James Thornber, stalker. The man on the right with the walking stick is the ponyman, John MacDonald. The other three men are the shooting party.

William Milne, on the left, photographed with his friends, smoking their pipes, playing cards and drinking 'Fine Old Scotch Whisky' on his farm of Northside near Skene in Aberdeenshire, in about 1900. Mabel Smith, an Aberdeenshire farmworker's daughter recalled card-playing in the early 1900s: 'Packs of cards were called The Devil's Books, but mother said it was just those who couldn't play cards who wouldn't have them in the house. Mother and my sister were very keen card players; one's right hand was at great risk when playing "Snap" with the two of them.'

The companion photograph shows the cardplayer's wives taking tea and sandwiches. Mrs Milne is pouring the tea.

Although both posed and perhaps deliberately tongue-in-cheek, these two photographs clearly demonstrate the differences between what were considered respectable leisure pursuits for men and women.

A dram given to the clippers to
celebrate the end of the sheep shearing at Buskhead Farm near Tarfside
in Glen Esk, Angus in 1967 – with
lemonade apparently available for
the less hardy.
Alexander Fenton, NMS

Spectators at the Dalserf Farmers Society Show in Lanarkshire, in 1928. Mabel Smith recalled the great Aikey Fair, near Old Deer in Aberdeenshire:

'For those in the vicinity there was 'Aikey Fair' held on a day in summer which became a recognised local holiday. It was a horse-fair still when we were at Philorth (Mabel's father worked on this farm from 1909 to 1915). The manager always went to it, and we used to have a P.C. (post card) of the Fair - a sea of horses - ... I was never at the Fair, but one of my girl cousins wouldn't have missed it for anything. To her it was a chance of meetin' in wi' her many relatives and acquaintances and gettin' the news. For that you'd nowadays go to the Turra (Turriff) Show.'

Dancing to the pipes at a fair in Campbeltown, Argyll, in about 1900. Judging from the looks of amusement and wonder on the onlookers' faces, they are admiring the skilled leg-work required to perform a dance such as a jig or a sailor's hornpipe.
Charles MacGrory, Campbeltown

An early film show in a school class-
room in Orkney in the 1950s. The
photograph was taken by Sandy
Wylie who went from island to
island showing films. On this particular evening he was showing a Bud
Abbot and Lou Costello film.
Sandy Wylie

Jane Gibson, aged 87, holding a
sickle and corn sheaf at Priory Farm,
Balmerino, Fife, in about 1900.
  She was almost certainly photographed in this way to lend interest
to the composition and give her dig-
nity, rather than because she was
expected to help much with the
harvest.
J C Dickie, Leuchars

AS OTHERS SEE US

The following chapter focuses on pictures of people which are very much posed, portrait photographs rather than documentary or action shots. Although the subjects of these photographs may be holding objects or animals, these are often only symbolic as they are rarely actually using them or working with them. Through their photographs it is possible to examine how people chose to portray themselves, and what they and the photographers judged worthy of recording. The horseman, for instance, would not dream of being photographed without his horse, nor would the shepherd be without his dogs: their animals are in a sense extensions of themselves, much loved, vital to their livelihoods and defining their occupations. Like animals, the objects we are used to working with also help us to feel more secure in front of the camera. Observe how much more relaxed are the people who are holding an object or an animal than are those who have nearly all opted to cross their hands or their arms in an attempt to find something to do with them.

Two examples also illustrate how the use of photographs as evidence can be of great value to the historian, but misleading if inadequately documented and researched.

The story of one photograph

The story of the identification of the photograph of Jane Gibson (pictured opposite) is particularly interesting, a good example of detective work and of how misleading wrongly identified photographs can be. The photograph was originally copied from an album belonging to Corstorphine Local History Society, and the woman was thought to be Ann Egan, an Irish woman, who had lived in Corstorphine. The photograph was published in a magazine in 1988 and recognised by Mrs J Cunningham from Fife as identical to one of her family photographs and of the same woman featured in two others. Mrs Cunningham started researching her family history and the Museum tried to date the photographs and find out more about Ann Egan.

Mrs Cunningham's researches revealed that the woman in the photograph was her great-grandmother, Jane Gibson, born on 12 December 1813 in the village of Creich in Fife. She married James Graham, a ship's carpenter, in December 1841. They had six children and in the 1871 census for the Gauldry-Balmerino District of Fife were registered as James Graham, gardener and Jane Gibson, housekeeper. They remained in the same area until their deaths at Priory Farm, Balmerino, James Graham in 1898, and Jane Gibson in 1902.

Ann Egan, a widow from Roscommon in Ireland appears in the 1851, 1861 and 1871 censuses. She was living in Corstorphine near Edinburgh throughout this period, with one or other of her children. In the Register of Deaths for 1885 she is listed as Ann Egan, widow of Patrick Egan, labourer.

Naomi Tarrant, NMS curator of costume, was able to say that one of Mrs Cunningham's family photographs, which showed a group of people including the old woman, could not have been taken before 1895 because of the particular style of the blouse worn by one of the women. The old woman was therefore definitely not Ann Egan.

We hope that someone may be able to tell us more about Ann Egan, perhaps produce a photograph of her, and explain how Jane Gibson's photograph came to be in the Corstorphine album.

Bothy Group Photographs

Photographs of bothy groups are unusual in that they show very clearly how people can sometimes choose to manipulate the photographer in order to produce the desired image of themselves. In many of these photographs the men are engaging in apparently odd activities. There is frequently a loaf of bread, usually being cut with a saw or an axe, or a kitchen pot with something unexpected inside it. A sack of meal or potatoes is also common, as are musical instruments, often a fiddle or a melodeon.

In these pictures the bothy men chose to use everyday objects as symbols of their lives, showing their independence, self-sufficiency and toughness, their hard living conditions and, above all, their strong sense of humour. Perhaps they were deliberately recreating the stereotypical view held of them. Of the dozens of photographs of bothy groups held by the Archive, only one shows the interior of a bothy, so the habit of displaying some of their contents provides us with visual evidence of the living conditions and pastimes of the bothy men to back up written and oral sources.

The pictures shown here encapsulate our reasons for taking photographs: as mementoes, as evidence of a particular identity or of belonging to a particular group of people, as historical or journalistic records, or even simply as a means of making a living. To the historian they are evidence of both change and continuity within families or communities, in social customs and in working practices. They provide clues to, and reminders of, the lives of some of the individuals who have lived and worked in rural Scotland.

Harvest-time, probably at Kilervan, Southend, Kintyre, in the mid-1920s.

The young women appear to have been helping fork oat sheaves onto carts. They are Nellie McSporran, Janet Ferguson and Katie MacMillan. The crochet-work woollen caps worn by Nellie and Janet were fashionable in the 1920s.

The Law family photographed on a cold windy day at Craighill of St Cyrus in Kincardineshire in the early 1900s. William Law was grieve at the farm. The family have dressed in their best clothes for the occasion. The two older girls are wearing bows in their hair matching their cotton dresses and the happy little boy an Eton collar and Glengarry: both very popular items of more formal dress for boys at the time. The entire family is wearing heavy leather boots, essential footwear worn indoors and out on a farm.

Duncan Keir, shepherd at Balimeanoch Farm on the south side of Loch Earn, Perthshire, with Chris, Witch and Bob around the 1960s.

This was one of the last photographs of Duncan Keir. His widow, Annie, treasured his family photographs, the shepherd's plaid which had belonged to his father before him, and some of the drawings he had made whilst at Drumvaich school near Doune in the early 1900s. The photographs were copied and the plaid and school drawings are now in the NMS collections.

An Angus cattleman, his wife and their rather reticent sons photographed in 1920, again in their best clothes. The Eton collar is still popular, as are the heavy boots worn by all but the mother and youngest boy. Women's fashions had undergone a considerable change between these two photographs, the First World War having contributed to the shortening of skirt lengths.

Bothy lads at the door of their bothy at Lundie Castle farm in Angus in 1927. They are: H Scott, R Buick and J Martin. The sacks tied around their legs helped protect their trousers from the mud and muck of the farm.

The bothy system was introduced in the late 18th century in Angus and the Mearns as an economical means of housing single farmworkers. It spread to parts of most of the eastern lowland counties, usually on the larger farms, during the 19th century, before decreasing at the end of the century and finally disappearing in the years following the First World War. Single or occasionally two-roomed bothies provided very basic accommodation where the farmworkers looked after themselves, the farmer providing each with a daily allowance of oatmeal and milk, and chaff for their mattresses.

Building sheaves into stacks in the stackyard of Kilervan Farm, near Southend, Kintyre, in the early 1920s. The men are: unknown, Duncan McCallum, John Reid, John Ferguson, Rob McSporran, roadman, and Andrew Ferguson. The spades were used for *keeping* the stacks: trimming the rough edges and rounding them off on top.

A group of fishergirls from Nairn in their best clothes on one of their Sunday days off in 1904. They are outside their lodging hut at the fish curing station of Gremista, near Lerwick in Shetland. They are, standing: Elsie Anne Cope, Libby Barron, Margaret Elizabeth MacIntosh, Libby –, and Margaret Wallace; seated: Nellie Bochel, Elsie MacIntosh and Margaret Ralph. They have painted the name *Glenerne* – the steam drifter they worked with – on the door of their hut to help give it an identity, in much the same way as photographs of groups of farm workers tend to show the name of the farm.

This informal group of farm workers was photographed outside the stables at East Inchmichael Farm, near Errol, Perthshire in 1919.

They are: John Robertson, another John Robertson, David Dow, Thomas Reddie, James Gibson with the cat, Alex Dowie and James Mackie. All the men are dressed in their everyday working clothes and tackety boots. James Gibson has very basic string nicky tams (straps, often of leather, used to help keep trousers clear of mud). The area in front of the stables was cobbled to prevent the ground from being churned up by the comings and goings of the horses.

Dave Hunter with his pair of horses at Leuchars Castle Farm, Leuchars, in Fife in 1926.

In the hierarchy of farm workers, the horsemen were right at the top and took much pride both in their horses and in their good handling of them. Dave Hunter has obviously spent some time grooming himself and his pair for the photograph. He is wearing a bright clean shirt and good trousers and jacket and has tied a neat little knot into the front of each horse's mane to keep it out of their eyes.

Alexander McColl with one of the horses for which he was responsible near Auchnangoul, by Inveraray, in about 1936.

He was woodman carter for the south portion of the Duke of Argyll's Inveraray estate. His engagement, which had started on 1 December 1928, included the following conditions of service: he was employed at a salary of 42 shillings per week, paid monthly; he was given occupation of French Farland cottage and its land which included grazing for one cow and follower (i.e. a calf), rent free. In the months of March to October he was expected to work nine hours a day, and four and a half hours on Saturday. From November to February, from daylight until dark, and to mid-day on Saturdays. He was allowed five paid holidays in the year - New Year's Day, two Fast Days, Empire Day and Inveraray Games Day. If the victim of an accident or off sick, he would have been paid for three days, after which his case would have been reviewed. These were relatively good conditions of service for the period.

Janet Umphray of Ham, wife of
Robert Peterson, seated knitting a
sock with needles probably made of
wood, outside her house on the
island of Foula, Shetland, in 1902.
The speed of her work comes across
clearly in the blurr of her right hand.
H B Curwen Collection

Mother and daughter enjoying the sun on the steps of their caravan at Crossmichael in Kirkcudbrightshire in the spring of 1948.

They belonged to a group of travelling people who spent the spring and summer working their way around the farms of Galloway, painting and whitewashing farm buildings, carts and implements. The neat covered wagons pulled by horses had been brought back into use during the war as petrol rationing had made it impossible for them to continue using their trailer caravans.

David Innes, Currie

The staff at Pusk farm near Leuchars in Fife. In common with many other groups of farm workers they have chalked up the name of the farm and the date on the door behind them. Unfortunately, none of them has so far been identified. All are wearing their everyday working clothes, although the little girl looks as though she has been tidied up for the occasion. She, the couple next to her and the young man being distracted by the cat, are the only ones entirely at ease with the camera.

Alexander Cumming and his wife Margaret Grant photographed with all their children in their garden in about 1910-12. The Cummings farmed the hill farm of Mains of Curr, Dulnain Bridge on the border of Inverness-shire and Morayshire.

The children are: John, Janet, Elspeth (Attie), Gregor, Flo, Alexander jnr (Allie), Don, General the dog, Madge, Mary, Grant and Violet.

The Cummings photographed a few years later in a photographer's studio with their two eldest sons John and Alexander.

The photograph was probably taken sometime during the First World War when the young men volunteered for the army. Families often have photographs taken in this sort of worrying situation as it may be the last time they are together.

John, who went on to become the managing director of an agricultural engineering company in Oxfordshire, was a Captain in the Seaforth Highlanders during the First World War, and a Major during the Second. Alexander was in the Royal Flying Corps during the First World War; but died, aged only twenty-six, in South Africa in the early 1920s.

A Ledingham, Grantown-on-Spey

'We will remember them'.
Until very recently the 11 November Remembrance Day two-minute silence was strongly respected everywhere. This is eighteen-year-old John (Jock) Hermiston with only a thin strip left to plough at the farm of Smedheugh near Selkirk in 1933. Jock worked at the farm for only a short time as he found it difficult to get Saturday afternoons off to allow him to play carpet bowls.

Local girls, one at least barefoot, relaxing during the peat cutting on the slopes of Carnan on the island of Mingulay in July 1905. At that time the small island had about 150 inhabitants. Today it is deserted except for the sheep that graze there. *Robert M Adam Collection, St Andrews University*

A dairymaid, possibly from Lanarkshire, photographed around the 1880s holding her luggie or milking-pail and her four-legged milking stool, the symbols of her occupation.

The objects, obviously held with some pride, helped to define her identity and showed her importance within her community. She is standing on a flagstone doorstep decorated, almost certainly by herself, with pipeclay designs. In the days when carpets, rugs and mats were a luxury saved for the best room these 'curly-wurlie' pipeclay designs were common on doorsteps and hearthstones. Some enthusiastic families even decorated their entire kitchen floor with them.

A carefully posed bothy group
photographed at Balmyle Farm near
Meigle in Perthshire in 1930. All the
men have found something to do
with their arms, either by crossing
them, resting one on the bench or
holding the dog.

57

ACKNOWLEDGEMENTS

The greatest debt goes to all those photographers and collectors of photographs who have over the years, by taking photographs, preserving them and donating them, created the photographic collections of the Scottish Ethnological Archive.

The following people and institutions very kindly agreed to the reproduction in this book of the photographs they had donated to the Archive. Many also provided a great deal of information:

Ted Allan
The late James Alston
Mrs May Barbour
Alan Barron
Steve Bichan
Andrew Broom
Robin Callander
Mrs M Campbell
Jemima B Cockburn
John Crawford
Jean Cunningham
    (Jane Gibson's great granddaughter)
Alex Cuthill
W G Dey FRIBA
John Dennison
William Diack
Lachlan F Dick
J Donaldson
David Duncan
Ian Fleming
Thomas Frame
William Gardiner
A Gilchrist
Rev. J L Goskirk
Alma Grant
R Allan Hamilton
David Hayes
Dr A E Henderson

Ian Larner
P K I Leith
The late A M MacDonald ARPS
The late Miss A M Mackay
Gus Maclean
Angus Martin
Tom Middlemass
David M Munro
The late I Petrie
John D M Robertson
Mrs Joyce M Sanderson (who now
    holds the photographic collection of
    her late father, Dr C W Graham of
    Edinburgh)
Anne M Scott
Neil Short
Mrs C Simpson (William Milne's
    granddaughter)
Eric Simpson
Katie Sproat
Iain Thornber JP DL
Bruce Walker
D Willis
Morven Wright
The MacGrory Collection, Argyll and
    Bute District Library
Auchindrain Museum, Inveraray
Biggar Museum Trust

Carloway Historical Society

Comunn Eachdraidh Bharraidh (Barra Historical Society)

Comunn Eachdraidh Nis (Ness Historical Society)

Fife Folk Museum, Ceres

Glenesk Folk Museum

Gorebridge and District Local History Society

Nairn Fishertown Museum

National Trust for Scotland – Angus Folk Museum, Glamis

The R M Adam Collection and the Valentine Archive, St Andrews University Library

Scottish Milk Marketing Board

Scottish Photography Archive, (Riddell Collection)

I would especially like to thank John Crawford, Alex Cuthill, William Gardiner and Angus Martin who went to a great deal of trouble to provide additional information.

I would also like to thank the following for their help, advice and expertise in the preparation of this book: Alan Borthwick, Hugh Cheape, Alistair Dodds, Lorna Ewan, Alexander Fenton, Stephen Gibson, May Goodall, Anne Grant, Colin Hendry, Mrs W Hinings, Margaret King, Andrew Kitchener, Susan Lamb, Eira Langler, Ian Larner, Gina Lesley, Andrew Martin, Doreen Moyes, Michael Piears, Anita Quye, Stephen Reid, John Shaw, Neil Short, Gavin Sprott, Geoff Swinney, Naomi Tarrant, Veronica Thomson, Elizabeth Wright, and most especially my colleagues Jenni Calder and Alison Cromarty whose idea it was, and who edited and designed it respectively.

DK

The following organisations may be of interest to those wishing to pursue a particular aspect of Scottish history:

Cairdean nan Taighean Tugha
(Friends of the Thatched Houses)
c/o 12 Buccleuch Street
Innerleithen
EH44 6LA

Economic and Social History
Society of Scotland
c/o Department of Economic
    and Social History
Edinburgh University
Edinburgh
EH8 9JY

Scottish Country Life Museums Trust
c/o National Museums of Scotland
York Buildings
Queen Street
Edinburgh
EH2 1JD

Scottish Industrial Heritage Society
c/o 129 Fotheringay Road
Glasgow
G41 4LG

Scottish Labour History Society
c/o 21 Liberton Brae
Edinburgh
EH16 6AQ

Scots Language Society
c/o 6 Cairn Walk
Cults
Aberdeen
AB1 9RF

Scottish Local History Forum
c/o Huntly House Museum
142 Canongate
Edinburgh
EH8 8DD

Scottish Oral History Society
c/o School of Scottish Studies
University of Edinburgh
George Square
Edinburgh

Scottish Records Association
c/o Scottish Records Office
General Register House
Waterloo Place
Edinburgh

Scottish Vernacular Buildings
    Working Group
c/o 19 York Place
Edinburgh
EH1 3EL

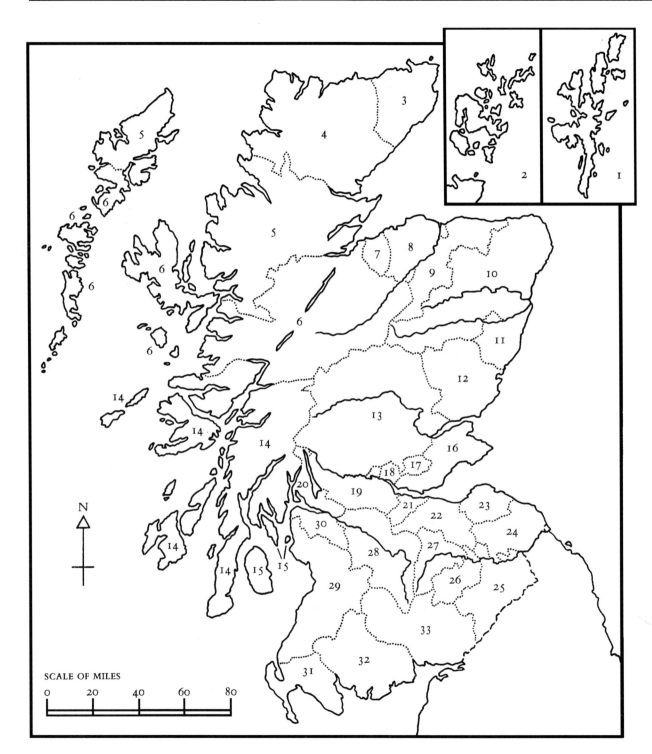

COUNTIES

1 Shetland Islands
2 Orkney Islands
3 Caithness
4 Sutherland
5 Ross & Cromarty
6 Inverness-shire
7 Nairn
8 Moray
9 Banffshire
10 Aberdeenshire
11 Kincardineshire
12 Angus
13 Perthshire
14 Argyll
15 Bute
16 Fife
17 Kinross-shire
18 Clackmannanshire
19 Stirlingshire
20 Dunbartonshire
21 West Lothian
22 Midlothian
23 East Lothian
24 Berwickshire
25 Roxburghshire
26 Selkirkshire
27 Peeblesshire
28 Lanarkshire
29 Ayrshire
30 Renfrewshire
31 Wigtownshire
32 Kirkcudbrightshire
33 Dumfriesshire